Directory of Irish Archives

THIRD EDITION

Edited by

Seamus Helferty and Raymond Refaussé

FOUR COURTS PRESS

This book was set
in 10.5 on 12 Times Roman.
Published in Ireland by
FOUR COURTS PRESS LTD
Fumbally Lane, Dublin 8, Ireland
e-mail: info@four-courts-press.ie
http:\\www.four-courts-press.ie
and in North America by
FOUR COURTS PRESS
c/o ISBS, 5804 N.E. Hassalo Street, Portland, OR 97213.

First edition, 1988
Second edition, 1993
Third edition, 1999

A catalogue record for this title
is available from the British Library.

ISBN 1–85182–468–5
ISBN 1–85182–469–3 Pbk

This book has been indexed by Helen Litton

Printed in Ireland
by Colour Books Ltd, Dublin

Contents

Introduction

If the period between the publication of the first (1988) and second (1993) editions of this directory was one of unprecedented development in Irish archives, the years since the publication of the second edition have not been without significant highlights. These have been the result of a combination of factors, the most notable being the ripple effect of the *National Archives Act, 1986* which contributed significantly to a heightened awareness of the value of archives; and a buoyant economy which provided the means to give concrete expression to that awareness through substantial improvements in provision for the preservation of archives. Within the national archival institutions, for example, there are major development or refurbishment projects in hand in both the National Archives and National Library; with the continuing substantial adaptation of the storage area in the National Archives premises and the opening by the National Library of the National Photographic Archive in Temple Bar as well as a new technical services building on the Kildare Street site.

Legislative provision for archives has been extended to local government with the inclusion in the *Local Government Act, 1994* of Section 65 which placed a statutory responsibility upon local authorities to manage and preserve their archives and to make them accessible to the public. The first step in implementing this new responsibility was a thorough and detailed survey of extant local authority archives, their condition and location, conducted by the National Archives on behalf of the Department of the Environment and carried out by four contract archivists. It is too early to say what shape the emergent local archives services will eventually take. Some authorities have followed the preferred course of the Department of the Environment in cooperating on the basis of regions defined by the *Local Government Act, 1991* and employing an archivist to move from one authority within the region to another, processing the backlog of archives within each authority. Other local authorities have taken an independent course in employing their own archivists. This would seem to offer the best option for the permanent preservation of local government archives. Professional custody of archives requires the employment of qualified professional archivists; not the transfer of a processed collection to the custody of a local library service which would seem to be the only alternative.

Other patterns which have emerged include the reorganisation and consolidation of the archives of some religious congregations, with material from houses and convents which are closing being transferred to a central custody. This is most notably the case with the the the Sisters of Mercy who supplied nine separate entries for the second edition but who are now developing the Mercy Central Archive in Dublin. Congregational, diocesan, and church archives generally, continue to be dynamic in the organisation of their archives and constitute approximately one third of the entries in this edition; without categorising as religious those educational institutions whose original *raison d'être* was undoubtedly such. A change will be noted with specific reference to diocesan archives where, with the exception of Clogher, the entries are exclusively Roman Catholic. This arises from an inclination within the Church of Ireland to encourage the transfer of archives to either the Representative Church Body Library in Dublin or the Public Record Office of Northern Ireland in Belfast; but it is inevitable that some material is retained in local custody. Given the general complexion of the entries for dioceses, it was not thought necessary to identify them individually as Roman Catholic, the entry for Clogher Church of Ireland Diocesan Archives being the only one distinguished by denomination.

There has been much reorganisation within the educational sector. The *Universities Act, 1987* introduced significant change in the organisation of universities as well as a great deal of confusion as to the nomenclature of those colleges which formerly constituted the National University of Ireland. While the university colleges at Cork and Galway straightforwardly, if rather laboriously, became the National University of Ireland, Cork, and National University of Ireland, Galway, respectively, the situation with St Patrick's College, Maynooth and University College Dublin is more complicated. The secular college at Maynooth has become the National University of Ireland, Maynooth. However, the pontifical college continues under the old name and has custody of the college archives as well as important collections of archives from the Irish colleges in Spain, most notably Salamanca. University College Dublin petitioned the government to retain its existing name as its primary identifier and, having been given permission, became University College Dublin, National University of Ireland, Dublin. It has not been thought necessary to use this full title in the entry for U.C.D. In general, an attempt has been made to give direction through the generous use of cross-references.

As well as attempting to gather as many new entries as possible for this edition, the categories of information within each entry have been extended, particularly to take cognisance of astounding technological advances within the last five years. It is not at all unusual for researchers to have the facility to contact a repository by post, telephone, fax and e-mail and, in addition, to be able to browse a website. While this is not universally the case, it is obviously useful to provide these contact details where applicable. Whatever other trends emerge in the management of archives in the near future, it is clear that e-mail will become a main route for research enquiries and that websites will provide an attractive and practical alternative to traditional guide publication.

While progress in telecommunications has been impressive, it has not as yet included any simplification of the system of telephone area codes, particularly when phoning in either direction between Northern Ireland and the Republic of Ireland. The editors hope that they have taken the most straightforward approach by including, along with telephone numbers, the area codes for the respective jurisdictions; but some further direction may be found helpful:

− to phone a Northern Ireland number from the Republic of Ireland, place 08 before the area code.

− to phone a Northern Ireland number from the United Kingdom, use the area code given.

− to phone a Northern Ireland number from outside Ireland and the U.K., drop 01 from the beginning of the area code and replace it with 00 44. The number for the Public Record Office of Northern Ireland, for example, would be 00 44 232 251318.

− to phone a Republic of Ireland number from anywhere outside the country, including Northern Ireland and the rest of the U.K., drop the 0 from the beginning of the area code and replace it with 00 353. The number for the National Archives, for example, would be 00 353 1 407 2300.

Certain conventions in relation to contact details have been carried over from previous editions, such as the practice of giving the designation of the person responsible for archives within an organisation rather than a personal contact. With regard to opening hours, it is evident from the most cursory glance that the majority of institutions require, or at least advise, an appointment. Even where this is not the case, prospective visitors to any institution should make contact in advance to check on the availability of archives and the necessity for any form of identification. A first-time visitor to most institutions will be given a reference interview, a procedure which will be greatly facilitated if the visitor is expected. By checking in advance, even where this is not stipulated, a researcher will avoid the frustration of a wasted journey caused by occasional closure or the withdrawal of material for repair or exhibition.

The *Guides* category of each entry is intended to indicate any published material, such as a guide to all or specific categories of the holdings of an institution, which will assist a researcher in deciding whether that institution is likely to have material of relevance to their research. General information leaflets available from an institution are mentioned where applicable. It should be assumed that most institutions will have a network of finding aids, however rudimentary, which may be consulted only in the institution itself.

Again, as with previous editions, this *Directory* lays no claim to be a comprehensive guide to Irish archives. Certain categories of organisation or collection have been excluded as being the focus of other published guides or surveys. Trade union records, for example, are described in Sarah Ward-Perkins *Select Guide to Trade Union Records in Dublin* (Irish Manuscripts Commission, 1996), the result of a survey conducted on behalf of the Irish Labour History Society; while the Business Records Survey based in the National Archives continues to identify the location and extent of business records throughout the country, with the results being reported in successive issues of *Irish Economic and Social History*, 10– (1985–). Reference to these categories of collection is made only where they have been transferred to a custodial institution which has supplied an entry for inclusion in this *Directory*.

The editors are indebted to Michael Adams and Martin Healy of Four Courts Press for their sustained interest in this project; to their colleagues in the Irish Region of the Society of Archivists and most particularly in the Representative Church Body Library and the Archives Department, University College Dublin; but most of all to those custodians, the majority of whom are neither permanent nor salaried and for whom archives is but one of many responsibilities, and who responded readily to a request to furnish information. Where there are obvious lacunae, the editors can only plead an inability to obtain a response from an organisation despite repeated attempts; and the constraints imposed by the primary motive to maintain this *Directory* as a reliable work of reference.

1   The Adelaide & Meath Hospital Dublin Incorporating the National Children's Hospital

Address   Tallaght
Dublin 24

Telephone   (01) 414 2000

E-mail   Karlmagee@AMNCH.ie

Enquiries to   The Archival Manager

Opening hours By appointment
and facilities

Guides   Karl Magee, 'New hospital, old records – the archives of the Adelaide & Meath Hospital Dublin incorporating the National Children's Hospital', *Irish Archives* 4, no. 2 (Autumn 1997)

Major collections

Minutes of various boards and committees of the Adelaide Hospital, 1838–, Meath Hospital, 1776–, and National Children's Hospital, 1956–.

Annual reports of the Adelaide Hospital, 1858–, Meath Hospital, 1864–, and National Children's Hospital, 1920–.

Adelaide Hospital and Meath Hospital, late 19th and early 20th century doctors' casebooks.

Records of the Federated Dublin Voluntary Hospitals, 1961–.

Memorabilia including photographs, paintings, sculpture, memorial plaques and medical instruments.

Oral history collection of interviews with retired members of staff from the Adelaide Hospital, Meath Hospital, National Children's Hospital and St Loman's Hospital.

2   Airfield Trust

Address   Airfield
Upper Kilmacud Road
Dublin 14

Telephone   (01) 298 4301

Fax   (01) 296 2832

Enquiries to	The Archivist
Opening hours	By arrangement

Major collections
Private family papers of the Overend family (Dublin), 19th century.

3   Alexandra College

Address	Milltown Dublin 6
Telephone	(01) 497 7571
Fax	(01) 497 4873
E-mail	alexcold@iol.ie
Website address	www.iol.ie/~alexcold/
Enquiries to	The Archivist/Librarian
Opening hours and facilities	9.00–4.00, Mon–Fri; appointment necessary; initial letter to the College Principal outlining research project; photocopying
Guides	Anne V. O'Connor & Susan M. Parkes, *Gladly Learn and Gladly Teach* (1984) is a history of the College with a bibliography of sources.

Major collections
College Council minutes, 1866–1930, and extracts from minutes, 1930–66.
Lady Principals' reports, 1930–45.
Committee of Education minute books, 1866–1911.
Alexandra School Committee of Education minutes, 1887–1939.
Alexandra College Registers of Proficiency and Progress, 1866–72, 1882–1914.
Alexandra College daily roll book, 1879–81.
Lady Superintendents' notes, 1876–86.
Finance Committee account book, 1882–1926.
Collection of College publications including the prospectus, 1866–76; Alexandra College Magazine, 1893–98; Alexandra College, Dublin, Jubilee Record, 1866–1916; and College calendars, 1879–1901.

4   All Hallows College

Address	Grace Park Road Dublin 9
Telephone	(01) 837 3745
Fax	(01) 837 7642
E-mail	ahallows@iol.ie
Website address	www.iol.ie/~ahallows
Enquiries to	The College Archivist
Opening hours and facilities	By appointment

Major collections

Correspondence between Catholic bishops and priests and the College of All Hallows, 1842–; correspondence is from Britain, USA, Australia, Canada, New Zealand, India, Mauritius, West Indies, Argentina and South Africa.

The early correspondence, 1842–77, has been microfilmed and is available in many overseas state and national libraries.

5   Allen Library

Address	Edmund Rice House North Richmond Street Dublin 1
Telephone	(01) 855 1077
Fax	(01) 855 5243
E-mail	allenlib@connect.ie
Website address	www.connect.ie/users/allenlib
Enquiries to	The Curator/Librarian
Opening hours and facilities	10.00–5.00, Mon–Fri; appointment necessary; photocopying

Major collections

Roll and examination books for O'Connell Schools.

Congregational material for the Christian Brothers.

Papers, photographs and other memorabilia relating to prominent Irish political and literary figures including Michael Collins, Roger Casement, Seán T. O'Kelly, Alice Milligan, Maud Gonne McBride, W.B. Yeats, Arthur Griffith, P.H. Pearse, Dr Kathleen Lynn and Eamonn Ceannt.

6   Allied Irish Banks plc

Address	3/4 Foster Place Dublin 2
Telephone	(01) 677 6721
Enquiries to	The Archivist
Opening hours and facilities	By postal enquiry from researchers providing suitable references; facilities by arrangement

Major collections

La Touche & Co. (1693–1870): small collection of account books and ledgers.

Provincial Bank of Ireland (1825–1966): Board minutes, circulars from head offices in London and Dublin, personnel registers.

Royal Bank of Ireland (1836–1966): Board minutes, annual accounts, personnel registers.

Munster Bank Ltd (1864–85): small collection of banking records.

Munster and Leinster Bank Ltd (1885–1966): Board minutes, head office circulars, personnel records.

7   Apothecaries Hall

Address	95 Merrion Square Dublin 2
Telephone	(01) 676 2147
Enquiries to	Apothecaries Hall
Opening hours and facilities	By appointment
Guides	M. Clark and R. Refaussé (eds), *Directory of Historic Dublin Guilds* (Dublin, 1993)

Major collections

Minutes of the Guild of Apothecaries (Guild of St Luke the Evangelist), 1747–1820.

Records of the Company of Apothecaries Hall: minutes, accounts, correspondence, lists of apprentices, assistants and certificate holders, 1791–; signatures to oaths of office, 1795–; lists of licentiates, 1859–; examination records, 1897–; attendance books, 1899–.

8   Ardagh & Clonmacnoise Diocesan Archives

Address	Bishop's House
	Longford
Telephone	(043) 46432
Fax	(043) 46833
E-mail	ardaghdi@iol.ie
Enquiries to	The Archivist
Opening hours and facilities	By appointment

Major collections

Ardagh Diocesan Archives contain considerable collections of papers which formed the correspondence of bishops during the 19th century. The papers begin *c.*1820, being noticeably incomplete up to 1853. The episcopate of George Conroy is represented by a small collection. The largest collection is that of Bartholomew Woodlock, 1879–95. There is very little material either extant or available after 1895.

9   Armagh County Museum

Address	The Mall East
	Armagh BT61 9BE
Telephone	(01861) 523070
Fax	(01861) 522631

E-mail	catherine.mccullough.um@nics.gov.uk/ greer.ramsey.um@nics.gov.uk
Enquiries to	The Curator
Opening hours and facilities	10.00–2.00, Mon–Fri

Major collections

T.G.F. Paterson collection: historical and genealogical manuscripts relating primarily to family pedigrees and local history with particular reference to County Armagh.

George Russell (AE) (1867–1935): small collection of papers including poems, letters and drawings.

Blacker daybooks: handwritten accounts by Colonel William Blacker (1775–1855) of contemporary events including the Battle of the Diamond, 1795, and of sermons preached by him.

Estate papers including records of the Charlemont Estate, 18th–19th centuries: leases, account books, maps and surveys.

Copies of records relating to County Armagh including: Hearth Money Rolls, 1664; Muster Rolls, 1630; Poll Book, 1753; census of Armagh City, 1770; First Armagh Presbyterian Church Registers, 1727–9, 1796–1809; abstracts from the rentals of the Archbishops of Armagh, 1615–1746; Manor of Armagh tenants, 1714; abstracts of depositions, 1641.

10   Armagh Diocesan Archives

Address	Ara Coeli Armagh BT61 7QY
Telephone	(01861) 522045
Fax	(01861) 526182
Enquiries to	The Diocesan Secretary
Opening hours and facilities	By appointment; reference required; photocopying

Major collections

Correspondence and other papers of Archbishops of Armagh, 1787–1927.

11   Armagh Observatory

Address   College Hill
                      Armagh BT61 9DG

Telephone   (01861) 522928

Fax   (01861) 527174

E-mail   meb@star.arm.ac.uk (Director)
                      jmf@star.arm.ac.uk (Librarian)

Website address star.arm.ac.uk

Enquiries to   The Director or Librarian

Opening hours 9.30–4.30, Mon–Fri; photocopying
and facilities

Guides   J. Butler & M. Hoskin, 'The Archives of Armagh Observatory', *Journal for the History of Astronomy* 18 (1987) lists archival material up to 1916 and is available on the website. J.A. Bennett, *Church, State and Astronomy in Ireland – 200 Years of Armagh Observatory* (Armagh Observatory, 1990). J. McFarland, 'The Rare and Antiquarian Book Collection of Armagh Observatory', *Irish Astronomical Journal* 33 (1990).

Major collections

Directors and astronomers papers: J.A. Hamilton (1748–1815), T.R. Robinson (1793–1882), J.L.E. Dreyer (1852–1926), E.J. Öpik (1893–1985) and E.M. Lindsay (1937–1974).

Correspondence relating to the Boyden Observatory, South Africa.

Astronomical observations of the positions of stars, planets and nebulae, 1782–1914.

Meteorological records from Armagh, 1785–.

Astronomical photographs taken with the Armagh Schmidt telescope, 1950–*c.*70, and the Armagh–Dunsink–Harvard telescope, 1950–74.

Estate papers relating to Derrynaught, Tullynure and Carlingford, 1790–1910, deposited with the Public Record Office of Northern Ireland (q.v.)

12   [Armagh] Public Library

Address	Abbey Street Armagh BT61 7DY
Telephone	(01861) 523142
Fax	(01861) 524177
E-mail	ArmRobLib@aol.com
Enquiries to	The Keeper
Opening hours and facilities	10.00–12.30, 2.00–4.00, Mon–Fri; at other times by appointment; photocopying, photography
Guides	*Catalogue of Manuscripts in the Public Library of Armagh* (1928)

Major collections

Papers of Anthony Dopping, Bishop of Meath (1682–97) relating to the diocese of Meath.

Correspondence of Lord John George Beresford, Archbishop of Armagh (1822–62).

Papers of William Reeves, Bishop of Down (1882–96) relating to Irish church history from the 5th to the 19th century.

Records of 17th and 18th century episcopal visitations.

Copies of Armagh primatial registers, 1362–.

13   Bank of Ireland

Address	Head Office Lower Baggot Street Dublin 2
Telephone	(01) 661 5933
Fax	(01) 661 5641
Enquiries to	The Group Secretary
Opening hours and facilities	Postal enquiry

Major collections

Archives of all major departments and offices of the Bank: Court of Directors including Court of Directors' Transactions or Minute Books, 1783–; Secretary's Office including Secretary's correspondence; Accountant General's Office including Account Books; Audit Office including reports on branches; Architect's Office including plans and photographs of branches; Branch Banks Office including memoranda from Head Office to branches and branch records; Law Agent's Office and Staff Office.

Extensive archives of the Hibernian Bank (1825–1958) and the National Bank (1834–1966) which merged with the Bank of Ireland.

14   Belfast Central Library

Address	Royal Avenue Belfast BTI IEA
Telephone	(01232) 243233
Fax	(01232) 332819
Enquiries to	The Irish and Local Studies Librarian
Opening hours and facilities	By appointment; photocopying
Guides	*Guide to the Irish and Local Studies Department* (Belfast, 1979)

Major collections

F.J. Bigger (1863–1926): 40,000 items. F.J. Bigger wrote and researched on local historical topics. He was editor of the *Ulster Journal of Archaeology*, but his interests were wide ranging and included all aspects of Belfast history, the United Irishmen, later nationalist movements and the revival of the Irish language. The collection includes his own correspondence and correspondence collected by him.

J.S. Crone (1858–1945): 10,000 items. J.S. Crone was President of the Irish Literary Society in London, founder and first editor of the *Irish Book Lover* and author of the *Concise Dictionary of Irish Biography*. The collection reflects these interests.

A.S. Moore (1870–1961): 1,000 items. Cuttings, pamphlets, indexes and compilations on local history, with special emphasis on industry.

A. Riddell (1874–1958): 5,000 items. Cuttings, indexes and compilations on social history and local biography.

19

Bryson and Macadam Collection: 44 manuscript volumes, late 18th and early 19th centuries, recording Ulster legends, poems and songs in the Irish language.

Literary collections including manuscripts, correspondence and diaries of Amanda McKittrick Ros, Forrest Reid, Sam Thompson, Lynn Doyle, St John Irvine and Alexander Irvine.

15   Belfast Harbour Commissioners

Address	Corporation Square Belfast BT1 3AL
Telephone	(01232) 554422
Fax	(01232) 554411
E-mail	info@belfast_harbour.co.uk
Enquiries to	The Senior Administrative Officer
Opening hours and facilities	By appointment only

Major collections
Records of various bodies relating to Belfast and its port, 1600–.

16   Birr Castle

Address	Birr County Offaly
Telephone	(0509) 20023
Fax	(0509) 20425
Enquiries to	The Secretary The Estate Office Ross Row
Opening hours and facilities	By appointment; access is restricted to those enrolled as Friends of Birr Castle Demesne; photocopying

Major collections
Correspondence and related papers of successive Earls of Rosse, 1595–; including correspondence and biographical material relating to Henry

Flood, 1765–*c.*1820, friend and political mentor of Sir Laurence Parsons, 2nd Earl, whose own papers, 1775–1841, include correspondence, political material, poetry, the history and genealogy of the Parsons family, as well as documents relating to the 1798 Rebellion, the Union, and his term as Joint Postmaster for Ireland, 1809–31.

Correspondence of the 3rd and 4th Earls, 1840–1909, particularly with other astronomers concerning Birr and other observatories; journals containing astronomical observations, and drafts for articles and speeches on astronomy; glass plate collection of Mary, Countess of Rosse, a pioneer photographer, 1854–60; letters and papers relating to Sir Charles Parsons, younger brother of the 4th Earl and inventor of the turbine engine.

Non–scientific correspondence of the 3rd to 7th Earls, 1840–1991, including correspondence of the 3rd Earl as President of the Royal Society, 1848–54, and of the 3rd and 4th Earls as Chancellors of Dublin University.

Estate office archives, 1604–1979, including maps, plans and drawings; leases and leasebooks; rentals, rent and other accounts; Irish Land Commission papers, 1874–1970; agents' correspondence, 1879–1965; and material relating to the families and Yorkshire estates of the wives of the 3rd, 4th and 5th Earls, the Wilmer Field family of Heaton Hall, Bradford; the Hawke family including papers of Admiral Sir Edward Hawke, 1st Lord Hawke and First Lord of the Admiralty, 1766–71; and the Lister Kaye family of Denby Grange, near Wakefield.

17 Bolton Library

Address	John Street
	Cashel
	County Tipperary
Telephone	(062) 61944
Enquiries to	The Custodian
Opening hours and facilities	By appointment
Guides	*Catalogue of the Cashel Diocesan Library* (Boston, 1973)

Major collections

Church of Ireland archives: parish records from the Cashel, Dundrum, Tipperary and Aherlow areas, 17th century–; Cashel Cathedral records, late 18th century–.

Miscellaneous ecclesiastical and secular manuscripts (deeds and legal documents, maps and plans, diaries, research notes and writings), and photographs, mainly 17th–19th century, but including two 13th century and one 14th century English liturgical manuscripts.

18 Carlow County Heritage Society

Address	Kennedy Street Carlow
Telephone	(0503) 33817
Enquiries to	The Curator
Opening hours and facilities	By appointment; photocopying

Major collections

Records of births, 1690–1900, marriages, 1690–1900, and deaths, 1860–1987, for County Carlow.

Tombstone inscriptions.

Purcell papers, 18th century–; Jackson papers, 17th–18th century.

Beresford papers.

Jennings archive.

19 Cashel & Emly Diocesan Archives

Address	Archbishop's House Thurles County Tipperary
Telephone	(0504) 21512
Fax	(0504) 22680
E-mail	cashelemly@tinet.ie
Enquiries to	The Archivist, St Patrick's College, Thurles, County Tipperary (q.v.)
Opening hours and facilities	By appointment, but originals are made available only in exceptional circumstances. Researchers are advised to consult the microfilm copies of the documents in the National Library, Kildare Street, Dublin. Permission is required to consult the material but is

readily given to bona fide researchers. Alternatively, facilities are provided to read the microfilm copies of the documents in St Patrick's College, Thurles; photo-copying

Guides   Calendars of the papers in Cashel Diocesan Archives are provided both in the National Library and in Thurles. Some of these have been published by Revd Mark Tierney in *Collectanae Hibernica* 9, 13, 16–20. Other material from the archives has been published by Revd Mark Tierney in *Collectanae Hibernica* 11 and 12 and by Revd Christopher O'Dwyer in *Archivium Hibernicum* xxxiii and xxxiv.

Major collections

Cashel Diocesan Archives contain large collections of the papers of the Archbishops of Cashel since the early 18th century. These papers are an important source for the history of the Archdiocese of Cashel as well as containing much material of national interest. The archives contain only a small number of items which are pre–18th century. The material is cat-alogued under the names of the various Archbishops of Cashel since the 18th century. At present the archives are accessible up to the death of Archbishop Croke in 1903.

The archives also contain the Skehan Index of Clergy of the Archdiocese of Cashel and Emly.

Further material belonging to the Cashel Diocesan Archives is in St Patrick's College, Thurles, where it may be consulted by arrangement. This material, the Skehan and Fogarty Papers, consists of two large col-lections of handwritten historical, biographical and genealogical notes relevant to the ecclesiastical and civil history of the Archdiocese of Cashel and surrounding area since the 18th century. The material is being computerised and listed with the intention of depositing copies in the Tipperary Joint Libraries, Thurles, County Tipperary (q.v.).

20   Castle Matrix

Address   Rathkeale
County Limerick

Telephone   (069) 64284

Fax   (069) 63242

E-mail	castlematrix@tinet.ie
Enquiries to	The Director
Opening hours and facilities	By appointment

Major collections

Castle Matrix was the headquarters of the International Institute of Military History and of the Heraldry Society of Ireland until 1991. The archives include: papers relating to the Irish 'Wild Geese' in the service of France and Spain, including a contemporary map of the Battle of Fontenoy and the order of battle, 1745, 1690–1820. Heraldic manuscripts including the 1572 Ordinary of Arms of Robert Cooke (Clarencieux King of Arms) comprising over 10,000 coats of arms. Documents relating to the Paris Commune, 1871.

Military archives including the papers of the rocket scientist Dr Clarence Hickman and papers relating to the air war in Europe and the Pacific, 1939–.

21   Cavan County Library

Address	Farnham Street Cavan
Telephone	(049) 31799
Fax	(049) 31384
E-mail	cavancountylibrary@tinet.ie
Enquiries to	The County Librarian
Opening hours and facilities	11.00–1.00, 2.00–5.00, Mon–Fri; photocopying
Guides	'Sources for Cavan Local History', *Breifne*, 1977–8. *Guide to County Cavan Local Studies Department*

Major collections

Copy charter of the town of Belturbet by George III; copy charter of the town of Cavan by James II, 28 February 1688.

Farnham Estate papers.

Maps of drainage and navigation of Ballinamore/Ballyconnell, passing from Lough Erne to the Shannon, 1846.

Ordnance Survey maps, 1835; Mornington Estate maps, 1853; Cavan-Leitrim Railway maps.

Collection of legal documents, leases, rentals, wills, for County Cavan, 18th and 19th century.

Barron Papers.

Registers, account & fee books, inspectors reports from Bailieboro Model School, 1860s–1900s.

Board of Guardian minute books, 1839–1921.

Rural District Council minute books, 1899–1925.

Newspaper cuttings from national and provincial newspapers on the '2nd' or 'New Reformation' in Cavan, with lists of those who conformed to the established church, 1824–6. Speeches and posters relating to the 1826 election in Cavan (microfilm).

Diary of Randal McCollum, Presbyterian Minister, Shercock, County Cavan, describing social conditions, 1861–71.

Photographs: Eason collection; Valentine collection; miscellaneous photographs and postcards relating to County Cavan, 20th century; railway photographic collection; Farnham family album.

Dean Richardson's *Leabhar na Nornaightheadh Comhchoitchienn* [Book of Common Prayer], *Caitecism na hEaglaise* and *Short History of the Attempts*.

22   Chester Beatty Library

Address	20 Shrewsbury Road
	Dublin 4
	from January 2000
	The Clock Tower Building
	Dublin Castle
	Dublin 2
Telephone	(01) 269 2386/269 5187
Fax	(01) 283 0983
E-mail	info@cbl.ie
Website address	www.cbl.ie
Enquiries to	The Librarian and Director
Opening hours and facilities	10.00–5.00, Tue–Fri, 2.00–5.00, Sat; photocopying; photography; microfilming; photocopying of manuscripts is not allowed

Guides　　　　　　　　A list of publications available for sale can be obtained from the Library or viewed on the website.

Major collections

The collection was the private library of Sir Alfred Chester Beatty (1875–1968), bequeathed on his death to the Irish people. The manuscript collection dates from several thousand years BC to the 20th century.

Manuscript holdings include:

Cuneiform clay tablets from the Berens collection.

Egyptian papyri: hieratic papyri containing love poems from *c.*1160 BC and a finely preserved Book of the Dead of the Lady Neskons.

Greek papyri include those collected by Wilfred Merton and the famous Biblical Papyri, eleven codices in all, 2nd–4th century AD.

Among the Coptic papyri are the texts of the lost books of the Manichaean faith and several biblical texts. There are small collections of Hebrew, Samaritan, Coptic and Syriac vellum manuscripts, mostly biblical.

Among the Syriac is a 5th century commentary on the Diatessaron by St Ephraim.

There is a small but significant collection of Western manuscripts, including a 12th century Walsingham Bible and several fine Books of Hours. The Slavonic manuscripts, also primarily biblical, are notable for their quality and illumination.

There are over 3,000 Arabic manuscripts in the collection covering every branch of religious and secular literature. The collection of Qurans includes a large number of early examples, including a 9th century example written in gold on blue vellum and a unique Quran written at Bagdad in 1001 by Ibn al–Bawwab, a celebrated calligrapher. The Persian manuscripts cover the whole range of painting, calligraphy and book arts and include a fine 14th century Shah–Namah.

The Indian section has many finely illustrated manuscripts in the Mughal style, including a chronicle of Akbar the Great. There are several Jain, Nepalese, Tamil, Kanarese and Sinhalese manuscripts.

The Burmese, Siamese, Tibetan and Mongolian collections number *c.*350 items and there are more than 40 Batak manuscripts from Sumatra, dealing mainly with magical subjects. The Chinese collection contains more than 170 hand–painted scrolls and albums, and 14 imperial jade books. In the Japanese collection there are *c.*100 scrolls and albums.

The Library also holds Chester Beatty's correspondence relating to the formation of the collection and the establishment of the Library, *c.*1910–68.

Administrative records of the Library, 1968–.

23   Church of Ireland College of Education, Research Area

Address	Upper Rathmines Road Dublin 6
Telephone	(01) 497 0033
Fax	(01) 497 1932
Enquiries to	The Principal
Opening hours and facilities	By appointment. Normally materials can only be made available during academic term time. Please write for details and an application form; photocopying; photography

Major collections

Kildare Place Society Collection: central administrative and financial records of the society; general, committee, parliamentary, publishing and inspectors' correspondence; correspondence between the Society and its schools; educational effects.

Church of Ireland Training College Collection: records of the College, 1884–, and some earlier records of the Church Education Society training institution. (Certain classes and ages of documents are closed to researchers.)

Other manuscript collections: Disestablishment correspondence, 1860s; Protestant Defence Association correspondence; Kildare Place Ex-Students Association in Northern Ireland collection, 1936–79.

Older printed books and textbooks: copies of textbooks and chapbooks published by the Kildare Place Society in the early 19th century, including those published in tablet or chart form, and a wide range of later 19th and early 20th century Irish textbooks.

24   Clare County Council

Address	New Road Ennis County Clare
Telephone	(065) 21616
Fax	(065) 20882

Website	www.clare.ie/
Enquiries to	The Archivist
Opening hours and facilities	By appointment

Major collections
Clare County Council minute books, 1899–1968.
Minute books of the Board of Health and Public Assistance, 1921–42.
Finance Committee minute books, 1906–38.
Agenda books, 1946–68.
Manager's Orders, 1942–66.
Personnel records, 1945–68.
Planning files, 1961–.

25   Clare County Library Local Studies Centre

Address	The Manse Harmony Row Ennis County Clare
Telephone	(065) 682 1616 (ext. 271)
Fax	(065) 42462
E-mail	clarelib@iol.ie
Website address	www.iol.ie/~clarelib
Enquiries to	The Local Studies Librarian
Opening hours and facilities	10.00–1.00, 2.00–5.30, Mon–Fri; photocopying

Major collections
Poor Law Records of County Clare, 1850–1922; Grand Jury Presentments, 1854–1900; minute book of the Borough of Ennis, 1699–1810; maps.

26   Clogher Diocesan Archives

Address	Bishop's House Monaghan
Telephone	(047) 81019
Fax	(047) 84773
Enquiries to	The Archivist
Opening hours and facilities	11.00–1.00, Mon–Wed; photocopying
Guides	Microfilm and catalogue in Public Record Office of Northern Ireland (q.v.)

Major collections
Papers of James Donnelly, Bishop of Clogher (1864–93).
Baptismal and marriage records for some parishes of the diocese to 1880.

27   Clogher Diocesan Archives [Church of Ireland]

Address	St Macartan's Cathedral Clogher County Tyrone BT76 0AD
Telephone	(016625) 48235
Enquiries to	The Dean
Opening hours and facilities	By appointment

Major collections
Clogher diocesan records: visitations, rural deans' reports, maps, 18th–20th century.
Clogher chapter lease book, 18th–19th century.
Clogher Corporation book, 1783.

28   Clonalis House

Address	Castlerea County Roscommon
Telephone	(0907) 20014
Enquiries to	The owner
Opening hours and facilities	By appointment
Guides	Gareth W. and J.E. Dunleavy (comps), *The O'Conor Papers: a descriptive catalogue and surname register of the materials in Clonalis House* (Madison, Wisconsin, University of Wisconsin Press, 1977)

Major collections

Major collection of *c.*100,000 manuscripts, 16th century–, including the works of Charles O'Conor of Belanagare.

29   Clonfert Diocesan Archives

Address	St Brendan's Coorheen Loughrea County Galway
Telephone	(091) 841560
Fax	(091) 841818
Enquiries to	The Bishop of Clonfert
Opening hours and facilities	By appointment

Major collections

Title deeds and legal documents concerning diocesan property, 1793–.

Visitation books, conference and synod books, registers of clergy.

Correspondence and papers of individual bishops, including letters to and from Rome, pastoral letters, and material concerning general diocesan administration. These papers date from the 1830s but little survives from before the 1880s.

30   Clongowes Wood College

Address	Naas County Kildare
Telephone	(045) 868202
Fax	(045) 861042
E-mail	clongowes@s-j.ie
Website address	homepage.tinet.ie/~clongowes
Enquiries to	The Rector/Archivist
Opening hours and facilities	Postal enquiry only; photocopying

Major collections
Complete register of pupils, parents or guardians, with addresses and fees, May 1814–.
Incomplete series of Journals of Prefects of Studies and of House Journals; academical exercises, mainly 1818–65; Rules for Masters and Rules for Pupils, with revised editions of both; registers of the Sodality of Our Lady and other pious organisations; minutes of the Social Study Club, 1913–25.
The Clongownian, annual, 1895–.

31   Cloyne Diocesan Archives

Address	Cloyne Diocesan Office Cobh County Cork
Telephone	(021) 811430
Fax	(021) 811026
E-mail	cloyne@indigo.ie
Enquiries to	The Archivist
Opening hours and facilities	Postal and telephone enquiries only

Major collections
Papers of bishops of the diocese.

32   Communist Party of Ireland

Address	43 East Essex Street Temple Bar Dublin 2
Telephone	(01) 671 1943
Fax	(01) 671 1943
Enquiries to	The National Chairperson
Opening hours and facilities	By appointment

Major collections

Miscellaneous collections of newspapers, leaflets, journals, photographs and posters relating to the Communist Party of Ireland and its international relations over 70 years.

Materials dealing with working life since 1913 in Dublin, Belfast and Cork.

Materials on the Irish involvement in the Spanish Civil War, 1936–9.

Large collection of materials relating to strikes and working class and small farmer struggles.

33   Companies Registration Office

Address	Parnell House 14 Parnell Square Dublin 1
Telephone	(01) 804 5254
Fax	(01) 804 5222
Enquiries to	The Information Unit
Opening hours and facilities	10.00–1.00, 2.15–4.30, Mon–Fri; company searches and photocopying

Major collections

Files relating to *c.*160,000 Irish companies and 3,000 external companies dating from the 1890s.

34 Contemporary Music Centre Ireland

Address	95 Lower Baggot Street Dublin 2
Telephone	(01) 661 2105
Fax	(01) 676 2639
E-mail	info@cmc.ie
Website address	www.cmc.ie
Enquiries to	The Music Librarian
Opening hours and facilities	10.00–1.00, 2.30–5.00, Mon–Fri
Guides	Information leaflet; information pack; newsletter *New Music News*

Major collections

Specialist collection of music by modern Irish composers. Includes music scores, sound archive and reference library relating to the compositions of Irish classical composers of the 20th century.

35 Córas Iompair Éireann

Address	Heuston Station Dublin 8
Enquiries to	The Registrar
Opening hours and facilities	Initial postal enquiry; subsequently by appointment; access is usually granted only to doctoral students; photocopying

Major collections

Minute books and committee minute books of the main constituent companies of CIÉ, 1840s–.

36   Cork Archives Institute

Address	Christ Church South Main Street Cork
Telephone	(021) 277809
Fax	(021) 274668
Website address	www.corkcorp.ie
Enquiries to	The Archivist
Opening hours and facilities	10.00–1.00; 2.30–5.00 Tue–Fri; by appointment; closed Mon; photocopying; photography
Guides	Introductory leaflet; annual accessions lists. Ann Barry, 'Sources for labour history in the Cork Archives Institute', *Saothar* 10 (1984). Marita Foster, 'Hurley emigrant letters', *Irish Roots* 3 (1992). Patricia McCarthy, 'Maritime Records in Cork Archives Institute', *Irish Archives* 2, no. 1 (1992); 'Sources for the study of the Great Famine held at the Cork Archives Institute', *Journal of the Cork Historical & Archaeological Society* 102 (1997); 'The archives of local government in the Cork Archives Institute', *Irish Archives* 3, no. 2 (1996). *The Poor Law Records of County Cork* (Cork Archives Institute, 1995). *Descriptive list of the papers of Liam Ó Buachalla* (Cork Archives Institute, 1994).

Major collections

Record holdings relate to all aspects of Cork history. These include official transfers of records from Cork Corporation, Cork County Council and various Urban District Councils. Records of defunct organisations include Boards of Guardians and Rural District Councils. Non–offical records include business archives, private papers, landed estate papers, and archives of trade unions, clubs and societies.

Cork Corporation archives include minute books and papers of the Borough Council, 1901–67; and minute books of the Cemetery, City Hall & Working Class Dwellings, Clothing, Fitzgerald Park, General Purposes, Hackney Carriage, Improvements, Law & Finance, Public Health, and Stocktaking Committees, 1878–1929.

Town Clerk's Department files include correspondence with central government departments and outside agencies concerning Corporation business; and correspondence relating to the appointment of the City Manager, 1929.

37   Port of Cork Company

Address	Harbour Office Custom House Street Cork
Telephone	(021) 273125
Fax	(021) 276484
E-mail	info@portofcork.ie
Enquiries to	The Secretary
Opening hours and facilities	By appointment; photocopying

Major collections

Records of the Cork Harbour Commissioners who became defunct in March 1997: minutes of Board meetings, 1814–; registers of arrivals and sailings, 1912–; Board members attendance books, 1913–; registers of conveyances, 1836–1927; bye–laws, 1822–; accounts, 1871–; pilotage licences, 1924–.

38   Cork Public Museum

Address	Fitzgerald Park Mardyke Cork
Telephone	(021) 270679
Fax	(021) 270931
Enquiries to	The Curator
Opening hours and facilities	11.00–1.00, 2.15–5.00, Mon–Fri; by appointment; photocopying

Major collections

A large collection of documents and photographs, 1900–22, including the MacCurtáin and MacSwiney papers.

39   Cork–Ross Diocesan Archives

Address	Diocesan Office
	Bishop's House
	Redemption Road
	Cork
Telephone	(021) 301717
Enquiries to	The Diocesan Archivist
Opening hours and facilities	Postal enquiry only; photocopying

Major collections

Correspondence, papers and pastorals of Bishops of Cork, 1763–, with pre–1763 correspondence complemented by microfilm copy documents from Propaganda Fide and Vatican Archives; register of ordinations, 1691; calendars of deanery conferences, 1847–, synods and synodal enactments, 1816–, and diocesan statutes; indexes of clerical appointments, 1691–; collection of theological addresses of Bishop William Delany.

Personal papers of Dean Dominick Murphy, compiler of annals of the diocese (1834–74); Canon John O'Mahony (1874–1911); and Archdeacon T.F. Duggan (1917–65).

Correspondence of Bishops of Ross, 1830–2, 1851–1935; register of constitutions, conferences, synods, clerical appointments and financial returns of Ross, 1820–1929; manuscript histories of the diocese to 1864 and 1867–77.

40   Crawford Municipal Art Gallery

Address	Emmet Place
	Cork
Telephone	(021) 273377
Fax	(021) 275680
Website address	www.synergy.ie/crawford/
Enquiries to	The Gallery Secretary
Opening hours and facilities	10.00–5.00, Mon–Sat; no admission after 4.45; photography

Guides   Information leaflets on request

Major collections
Material from the Cork School of Art library, dating from the mid–19th century, including many large portfolios on architecture and the decorative arts. Material relating generally to art in Cork in 19th century. Minute books of the Technical Instruction Committee (later the Vocational Education Committee) and incomplete student registers, 19th–20th centuries. Diaries relating to the Gibson family, early 19th century; John Hogan architectural sketchbook, *c.*1830; 19th century continental lace and lace patterns.

41   De La Salle Brothers

Address	Castletown
	Portlaoise
	County Laois
Telephone	(0502) 32359
Enquiries to	The Archivist
Opening hours and facilities	Postal enquiry only; photocopying

Major collections
Material relating to the history of the congregation in Ireland.

42   Derry City Council
Heritage & Museum Service

Address	Harbour Museum
	Harbour Square
	Derry BT48 6AF
Telephone	(01504) 377331
Fax	(01504) 377633
Enquiries to	The Archivist
Opening hours and facilities	9.00–1.00, 2.00–5.00, Mon–Fri; by appointment; photocopying

Major collections

Archives of Derry Corporation including minute books, 1673–1969; correspondence files and letter books, 1849–1969; legal documents, 1679–1969; architectural drawings, 1877–1969; maps, 1830–1930; war memorial registers, 1926.

Private collections relating to Gwyn's Institution, 1838–1945; Tillie & Henderson's Shirt Factory, 1907–43; the City Factory, 1865–1965; Prior's Chemist, 1898–1947; Port and Harbour Commissioners, 1853–1944; A.A. Watt & Company Ltd, 1833–88; Irish Transport & General Workers' Union, 1955–69; Derry Trades Council, 1964–92; Northern Ireland Civil Rights Association, 1969–75; Londonderry & Lough Swilly Railway Company, 1889–1917; Great Northern Railway Company, 1880–93; Strabane & Letterkenny Railway Company, 1906; Buncrana & Carndonagh Light Railway Company, 1883–4; Derry Bridge Club, 1945–63; Alpha Tennis Club, 1955–67; Cooke family, 1832–1909; Bridget Bond, 1970–76; Kathleen Coyle, 1923–52; Jack Scoltock, 1990–96; Green Circle Players, Columcille Players and St Columb's College Union Dramatic Society, 1947–90.

43   Derry Diocesan Archive

Address	9 Steelstown Road Derry BT48 8EU
Telephone	(01504) 359809
Fax	(01504) 359809
Enquiries to	The Archivist
Opening hours and facilities	By appointment; photocopying

Major collections
Records of the diocese, 1939–.

44   Discalced Carmelites (Irish Province)

Address	St Teresa's Church Clarendon Street Dublin 2

Telephone	(01) 671 8466
Fax	(01) 671 8462
Enquiries to	The Provincial Secretary
Opening hours and facilities	Postal or telephone enquiry

Major collections

Material relating to the history of the Carmelite Community at Wormwoodgate Chapel, 1707–57, Stephen Street Chapel, 1757–97, and Clarendon Street Church, 1797–.

History of the various foundations made from Clarendon Street to elsewhere in Ireland and overseas.

45   Dominican Provincial Archives

Address	St Mary's Priory Tallaght, Dublin 24
Telephone	(01) 404 8100
Fax	(01) 459 678
Enquiries to	The Provincial Archivist
Opening hours and facilities	By appointment or by postal enquiry; photocopying

Major collections

Correspondence and papers of Dominican superiors and individuals, 1820–1922.

Collections of notes on Irish Dominican history by several historians of the Order.

Account books of many Irish convents.

Archives of the Dominican College of Lisbon.

Newscuttings, sermons and publications of members of the Province.

Chapter legislation, 1720–.

Books of reception and profession.

46   Dominican Sisters (Congregation of the Irish Dominican Sisters)

Address	5 Westfield Road Harold's Cross Dublin 6W
Telephone	(01) 492 3430
Fax	(01) 492 3470
E-mail	horganop@iol.ie
Enquiries to	The Archivist General
Opening hours and facilities	By appointment; photocopying

Major collections

Material concerning the growth and activities of the congregation, 1644–, with special emphasis on the period, 1719–. Includes relations internal to the Dominican Order, with ecclesiastical authorities and other congregations; relating to the Sisters' involvement with all levels of education, primary, secondary, third level and ecumenical; and other apolostic ministeries undertaken by the Sisters in Ireland, South Africa, Portugal, Louisiana, Argentina, Brazil and Bolivia.

47   Donegal County Library County Archive Centre

Address	The Courthouse Lifford County Donegal
Telephone	(074) 21968
Fax	(074) 26402
E-mail	dglcolib@iol.ie
Enquiries to	The Assistant Librarian, Local Studies
Opening hours and facilities	By appointment; photocopying; photography

Major collections
Boards of Guardians records for Ballyshannon, Carndonagh, Donegal, Dunfanaghy, Glenties, Letterkenny, Milford and Stranorlar, 1840s–1923.
Minutes of County Council committees and miscellaneous Council records.
District Council records (10 districts), 1899–1925.
Small collection of private records including estate papers and school records.

48   Donegal County Museum

Address	High Road Letterkenny County Donegal
Telephone	(074) 24613
Fax	(074) 26522
Enquiries to	The Curator
Opening hours and facilities	Written application required for permission to consult archives; photocopying

Major collections
Records of the Lough Swilly Bus & Rail Company [Londonderry & Lough Swilly Bus & Rail Company], early 20th century.
Archives of the Archaeological Survey of Donegal.

49   Down & Connor Diocesan Archives

Address	73a Somerton Road Belfast BT15 4DJ
Telephone	(01232) 776185
Enquiries to	The Archivist
Opening hours and facilities	By appointment; photocopying

Major collections
Correspondence of Bishop McMullan and Revd William McMullan, 1803–26.
Bishop Cornelius Denvir correspondence, 1835–65.
Archbishop William Crolly of Armagh correspondence, 1835–49.
Bishop Daniel Mageean correspondence, 1929–62.
Bishop William Philbin correspondence, 1962–82.

50   Down County Museum

Address	The Mall Downpatrick County Down BT30 6AH
Telephone	(01396) 615218
Fax	(01369) 615590
Enquiries to	The Keeper of Collections
Opening hours and facilities	11.00–5.00, Tue–Fri; 2.00–5.00, Sat; photocopying; photography

Major collections
The collections in the museum relate to County Down from the prehistoric period to the present and include documents associated with the collections: certificates, minute books, maps and plans.
Photographic archive.

51   Drogheda Corporation

Address	Fair Street Drogheda County Louth
Telephone	(041) 983 3511
Fax	(041) 983 9306
E-mail	tclerk@droghedacorp.ie
Enquiries to	The Town Clerk
Opening hours and facilities	9.00–5.00, by appointment; photocopying

Major collections
Charters: James II, 1687; William III, 1697; George I, *c.*1725; William IV, 1833.
Council Book (minutes), October 1649–.
Freedom Books, 1690–.
Maps: Newcomen's map of Drogheda, 1657; Ravell's map of Drogheda, 1749; Skinner and Taylor's map of Drogheda, 1778; Greene's map of Drogheda, 1878.

52 Drogheda Port Company

Address Maritime House
The Mall
Drogheda

Telephone (041) 983 8378/983 6026

Fax (041) 983 2844

Enquiries to The Secretary & Chief Executive

Opening hours 9.00–5.00, Mon–Thur; 9.00–4.45, Fri;
and facilities photocopying; photography

Major collections
Minute books, 1790–.

53 Dromore Diocesan Archives

Address Bishop's House
Newry
County Down

Telephone (01693) 62444

Fax (01693) 60496

Enquiries to The Bishop of Dromore

Opening hours By appointment; photocopying
and facilities

Major collections
Correspondence and papers of bishops, 1770–.
Records of baptisms, marriages and deaths for each parish, 1926–.
Other diocesan and parish papers.

54   Dublin City Archives

Address	City Assembly House
	58 South William Street
	Dublin 2
Telephone	(01) 677 5877
Fax	(01) 677 5954
Website address	www.iol.ie/resource/dublincitylibrary
	www.dublincorp.ie
Enquiries to	The Archivist
Opening hours and facilities	10.00–1.00, 2.00–5.00, Mon–Fri; appointment essential; photocopying; photography
Guides	Sir John T. and Lady Gilbert (eds), *Calendar of Ancient Records of Dublin* (19 vols., Dublin, 1889–1944); Philomena Connolly and Geoffrey Martin (eds), *The Dublin Guild Merchant Roll* (Dublin, 1992); Colm Lennon and James Murray (eds), *The Dublin City Franchise Roll* (Dublin, 1998); Jane Ohlmeyer and Eamonn Ó Ciardha (eds), *The Irish Statute Staple Books* (Dublin, 1998); introductory leaflets.

Major collections

Dublin City Charters (102 items), 1171–1727; medieval cartularies, including Liber Albus and Chain Book of Dublin; Dublin City Assembly Rolls, 1447–1841; board of aldermen, 1567–1841; sheriffs and commons, 1746–1841; Tholsell Court of Dublin, 16th–18th century; Dublin city treasurer's accounts, 1540–1841; freedom records, 1468–1918; city surveyor's maps, 1695–1827; records of some trade and religious guilds to 1841; Wide Streets Commission, 1757–1849; Paving Board, 1774–1840; charitable committees, including Mansion House Fund for Relief of Distress in Ireland, 1880; Rathmines and Rathgar township, 1847–1930; Pembroke township, 1863–1930; Civics Institute of Ireland, 1918–60.

Minutes and reports of Dublin City Council, 1841–; photographic collection including Liffey Bridges and North Strand bombing; records of Dublin Corporation committees and departments, 1840–1968.

55   Dublin Corporation Gilbert Library

Address	138/142 Pearse Street Dublin 2
Telephone	(01) 677 7662
Fax	(01) 671 4354
E-mail	dubcoll@iol.ie
Enquiries to	The Librarian
Opening hours and facilities	10.00–1.00, 2.15–5.30, Mon–Thurs; 10.00–1.00, 2.15–5.00, Fri; 10.00–1.00, 1.45–4.30, Sat; photocopying; photography; microfilming
Guides	Douglas Hyde & D.J. O'Donoghue (comps), *Catalogue of the Books & Manuscripts comprising the Library of the late Sir John T. Gilbert* (Dublin, 1918)

Major collections

286 manuscripts and transcripts of manuscripts, collected by, or transcribed for, Sir John T. Gilbert in connection with his work on the history of the City of Dublin and on Irish history. The Robinson MSS, *c.*1740–60, the notebooks and other documents of an Irish judge, are of interest in that they deal with notable law cases in which Mr Justice Robinson was involved; the collection of letters addressed to Richard Caulfield, 1848–60, cover topics connected with Irish topography and genealogy; James Goddard's 'Complete abstract of Deeds belonging to the Guild of St Anne' includes material on Dublin parishes and trade guilds. Transcripts include the Assembly Rolls of Dublin, 1660–1803, charters and documents of the Guild of the Holy Trinity or Merchant Guild of Dublin 1438–1824, and other guilds of the city; and a transcript of the Book of Charters belonging to the City of Dublin. Some transcripts are of documents which have since been destroyed or disappeared (e.g. copies of letters on state affairs in Ireland, from the Phillipps Collection—the originals were destroyed in a fire in 1711).

Dublin County Council *see* Fingal County Archives

56   Dublin Diocesan Archives

Address	Archbishop's House Drumcondra Dublin 9
Telephone	(01) 837 9253
Fax	(01) 836 8393
Enquiries to	The Archivist
Opening hours and facilities	9.30–1.00, 2.00–5.00, Mon–Fri; by appointment; photocopying; photography
Guides	Calendars of the collections are available until 1880. Calendars of the papers of Archbishop Murray (1823–52) have been published in *Archivium Hibernicum* xxxv–ixlii. For a general overview see David C. Sheehy, 'Dublin Diocesan Archives – an introduction', *Archivium Hibernicum* xlii (1987)

Major collections

Papers of the Roman Catholic archbishops of Dublin, *c.*1750–.

Papers of bishops (auxiliary), priests and lay persons, 1820–.

Diocesan (Chapter) records, 1729–.

Minutes of meetings of bishops, 1829–49; 1882.

Combined surviving records of the Catholic Board, the Catholic Association and the Repeal Association, 1806–47.

Papers of Dr Bartholomew Woodlock, rector of the Catholic University, 1854–79.

Records of Holy Cross College, Clonliffe, 1867–1946.

57   Dublin Port Company

Address	Port Centre Alexandra Road Dublin 1
Telephone	(01) 855 0888
Fax	(01) 855 0487
E-mail	dubport@dublin-port.ie
Enquiries to	The Archivist

Opening hours   10.00–5.00, Wed; by appointment; photocopying
and facilities

Major collections
Letters and documents, early 1860s–. Maps, early 1800s–. General ledgers,
  1801–. Records of employees, early 1900s–. Archives of the Customs
  House Docks, 1830s–, and of the Engineer's Department, 1905–.
  Arrivals and sailings, early 1930s–. Photographs of activity in the port
  and newscuttings concerning the port

58   Dublin Writers' Museum

Address   18 Parnell Square North
              Dublin 1

Telephone   (01) 872 2077

Fax   (01) 872 2231

E-mail   enterprises@dublintourism.ie

Enquiries to   The Curator

Opening hours   10.00–5.00, Mon–Sat; 11.00–5.00, Sun & public
and facilities   holidays; access to archives by appointment only

Major collections
Papers relating to Cornelius Ryan, Geoffrey Phibbs, Norah McGuinness,
  Bram Stoker and Lennox Robinson.

59   Dundalk Harbour Commissioners

Address   Quay Street
              Dundalk

Telephone   (042) 34096

Fax   (042) 35481

Enquiries to   The C.E.O.

Opening hours   9.00–5.00, Mon–Fri; photocopying; photography
and facilities

Major collections
Minute books, 1844– (some gaps); miscellaneous account books, 1850s–;
  wages books, 1908–; arrivals books, 1916–.

60 Dun Laoghaire–Rathdown County Council

Address	County Hall Marine Road Dun Laoghaire County Dublin
Telephone	(01) 205 4743/ 205 4700
Fax	(01) 280 6969
E-mail	gp@dlrcoco.ie
Website address	www.dlrcoco.ie/
Enquiries to	The Senior Staff Officer, General Purposes
Opening hours and facilities	Appointment necessary; photocopying

Major collections

Archives of Dun Laoghaire Corporation, 1930–73, including archives of the townships and urban district councils of Blackrock, Dalkey, Killiney-Ballybrack and Dun Laoghaire, mid-19th century–1930; records of the Dean's Grange Joint Burial Board.

Archives of that area of the former Dublin County Council now within the jurisdiction of Dun Laoghaire–Rathdown County Council are in the custody of Fingal County Archives (q.v.).

61 Dunsink Observatory

Address	Castleknock Dublin 15
Telephone	(01) 838 7911/838 7959
Fax	(01) 838 7090
E-mail	astro@dunsink.dias.ie
Enquiries to	The Director
Opening hours and facilities	By appointment; photocopying; photography

Miscellaneous astronomy documents, 1790–1850. Correspondence and minutes, 1947–87, held at Dublin Institute for Advanced Studies, 10 Burlington Road, Dublin 4

62   Elphin Diocesan Archives

Address	Diocesan Office St Mary's Sligo
Telephone	(071) 62670
Fax	(071) 62414
Enquiries to	The Diocesan Secretary
Opening hours and facilities	By appointment; photocopying

Major collections
Correspondence of Bishops Laurence Gillooly, John Clancy, Bernard Coyne, Edward Doorly and Vincent Hanly, 1858–1970. Some historical data on parishes in Elphin Diocese.

63   Erasmus Smith Trust Archives

Address	Danum Zion Road Rathgar Dublin 6
Telephone	(01) 492 2611
Fax	(01) 492 4427
E-mail	staffhsd@tinet.ie
Enquiries to	The Archivist
Opening hours and facilities	Enquiries by post, telephone, fax or e-mail

Major collections

Administrative records of 'The Governors of the Schools founded by Erasmus Smith Esq' including: legal papers, 1671–1959; accounts, 1673–c.1970; minutes of the Board of Governors, 1674–c.1970; material relating to scholarships, exhibitions and appointments in Trinity College, Dublin, 1712–1951; minutes of the Standing Committee, 1803–1923; letter books, 1810–1929 and correspondence, 1850–c.1970.

Records of the Trust's estates including: maps, 1776–1920; land agents' letter books, 1862–1911; Irish Land Commission papers, 1889–1933. Southern Estates leases and property deeds, 1672–c.1940; valuations, c.1815–1900; rentals, 1836–1923; and correspondence, 1860–1914. Western Estates leases and property deeds, 1667–c.1940; rentals, 1843–c.1900; and correspondence, 1859–1930.

Records of the Trust's grammar schools: Ennis Grammar School, 1720–1940; Galway Grammar School, 1859–1962; Drogheda Grammar School, 1864–1950; Tipperary Grammar School, 1866–1930; The High School, Dublin, 1870–1970.

Records of the English Schools [primary schools funded by the Trust and found throughout Ireland] including maps, plans and leases, 1810–c.1900; masters' and inspectors' reports, 1853–95; and correspondence, 1855–1947.

Material relating to secondary schools aided by the Trust including: Christ's Hospital, London, 1673–c.1930; King's Hospital [The Blue Coat School], 1807–1941; and Brunswick Street School, Dublin, 1871–1903.

64   Electricity Supply Board Archives

Address	Parnell Avenue Harold's Cross Dublin 6
Telephone	(01) 604 2132
Fax	(01) 604 2133
Enquiries to	The Archives Manager/Team Leader Archives
Opening hours and facilities	9.30–12.30, 2.00–4.00, Mon–Fri

Major collections
Archives relating to the history and development of electricity supply in
Ireland with particular reference to the Rural Electrification Scheme and
to individual power stations. Film, photographs and memorabilia. Oral
history collection of interviews with retired members of staff.

65   Fermanagh County Museum

Address   Castle Barracks
Enniskillen
County Fermanagh

Telephone   (01365) 325000

Enquiries to   The Museum Officer

Opening hours   9.00–1.00, 2.00–5.00, Mon–Fri;
and facilities   photocopying; photography

Major collections
Local Government: County Fermanagh landholding and sales posters;
County Assize proclamations.
Genealogy: correspondence of Lady Dorothy Lowry–Corry, 1931–5;
family records of Canon W.H. Dundas (d. 1941). 17th century documents: appointment of Hamilton as Governor of Enniskillen, 1689; letter
from Schomberg to Wynne, 1689; commission of Major J. Folliott as
major in the dragoons, 1689.
Ephemera dealing with entertainment, sport, politics, religion and organizations in County Fermanagh.

66   Fianna Fáil

Address   13 Upper Mount Street
Dublin 2

Telephone   (01) 676 1551

Fax   (01) 678 5690

E-mail   info@fiannafail.ie

Website address   www.fiannafail.ie

Enquiries to	The General Secretary
Opening hours	Appointment necessary; letter of reference required; photocopying
Guides	Eunan O'Halpin, 'Parliamentary discipline and tactics: the Fianna Fáil archives, 1926–32', *Irish Historical Studies* xxx, no. 120 (1997)

Major collections
Administrative records of General Secretaries and Headquarters, 1926–, but including some material preceding the foundation of the Party.
Minute books of the National Executive, Parliamentary Party and Committees.
Material relating to Ard Fheiseanna, 1927–92; and to elections, 1926–87.
Posters, newspaper cuttings, and Party publications, 1926–80s.
Material relating to Seán Lemass and the reorganisation of Fianna Fáil, 1954–7.

67   Fingal County Archives

Address	Library Headquarters 11 Parnell Square Dublin 1
Telephone	(01) 872 7777 ext.2864
Fax	(01) 873 2021
E-mail	fincolib@iol.ie
Website	www.iol.ie/~fincolib/
Enquiries to	The Archivist
Opening hours	10.00–1.00, 2.00–4.30, Mon–Fri; appointment necessary; photocopying
Guides	Introductory leaflets

Major collections
Records of Dublin County Council, 1898–1993; records of rural and urban district councils including Dublin North, 1901–30, Dublin South, 1899–1930, and Howth, 1918–40. Grand Jury records, 1818–98.

Records of the Dublin Board of Public Health, 1930–42, and Dublin
County Committee of Agriculture and Technical Instruction, 1908–72.
Records of Balbriggan Town Commissioners, 1860–1995.
Records of Townpike Roads including Dublin to Dunleer, 1775–1856;
Dublin to Mullingar, 1792–1856; Dublin to Malahide, 1826–55;
Dublin to Carlow, 1829–59; Dublin to Navan, 1800–48; Dublin to
Drogheda, 1849–55; and Dublin to Knocksedan, 1798–1856.
Private collections including records of Cloghran Stud Farm, 1954–89; and
records of the Cuffe family of Swords, 1797–1933.

68   Franciscan Library, Killiney

Address   Dun Mhuire
Seafield Road
Killiney
County Dublin

Telephone   (01) 282 6760/ 282 6091

Fax   (01) 282 6993

Enquiries to   The Archivist

Opening hours and facilities   By appointment; photocopying

Guides   G.D. Burtchaell and J.M. Rigg, *Report on Franciscan manuscripts preserved at the Convent, Merchants' Quay, Dublin* (Dublin, Royal Commission on Historical Manuscripts, 1906). M. Dillon, C. Mooney OFM, P. de Brún, *Catalogue of Irish manuscripts in the Franciscan Library, Killiney* (Dublin Institute for Advanced Studies, 1969). C. Mooney OFM, 'Franciscan Library, Killiney: a short *guide'*, *Archivium Hibernicum* xviii (1955), 150–6. C. Schmitt OFM, 'Manuscrits de la "Franciscan Library" de Killiney', *Archivum Franciscanum Historicum 57* (1964), 165–90. Ignatius Fennessy OFM, 'The B Manuscripts in the Franciscan Library, Killiney' in B. Millett and A. Lynch (eds), *Dún Mhuire, Killiney, 1945–95* (Dublin, 1995), 150–215

Major collections

Gaelic manuscripts, 11th–20th century, including 'Psalter of St Caimin', Liber Hymnorum, Martyrology of Tallaght (LL) and Annals of the Four Masters (to 1169); Irish Franciscan manuscripts, 17th–20th century, including papers relating to Irish Franciscan houses in Ireland and in Europe, and collections such as the Wadding Papers; Irish historical manuscripts 17th–20th century, such as the Hayes Papers on the Veto Question; Franciscan historical and theological papers, 15th–17th century.

69   The Gaelic Athletic Association Museum

Address	Croke Park Dublin 3
Telephone	(01) 855 8176
Fax	(01) 855 8104
Enquiries to	The Museum Administrator
Opening hours and facilities	9.30–5.00, Sun–Sat, May–Sept; 10.00–5.00, Tue–Sat, 12.00–5.00, Sun, Oct–Apr;

Major collections

A large collection of documents, memorabilia and photographs from the foundation of the Association in 1884 to the present, including minutes of meetings, programmes and printed matter.

Much of the collection is on display to the general public. An archive, and a photographic and reference library will be open to the public in the near future.

70   Galway County Libraries

Address	Island House Cathedral Square Galway
Telephone	(091) 562471
Fax	(091) 565039
E-mail	gallibr@indigo.ie
Enquiries to	The Executive Librarian

Opening hours   9.30–1.00, 2.00–5.00, Mon–Fri; photocopying
and facilities

Major collections
Estate papers: O'Kelly of Castlekelly; Blakes of Ballyglunin; some encumbered estates material.
Board of Guardian minutes: Ballinasloe, 1913–21; Clifden, 1849–1913; Galway, 1839–1921; Gort, 1844–1921; Loughrea, 1840–1905; Mountbellew, 1850–1912; Tuam, 1839–1921.
Rural District Council minutes: Ballinasloe, 1909–19; Clifden, 1899–1925; Gort, 1899–1924; Galway, 1904–21; Mountbellew, 1899–1913; Portumna, 1900–25; Tuam, 1917.
Galway Hospital minutes and accounts, 1892–1922; Galway County Board of Health minutes, 1922–39; Clonbrock Dispensary minutes, 1852–98; Galway County Council rateable valuations, 1900–30.

71   Galway Diocesan Archives

Address   The Cathedral
Galway

Telephone   (091) 563566

Fax   (091) 568333

Enquiries to   The Archivist

Opening hours   By appointment
and facilities

Major collections
Matters dealing with Galway Diocese.
Documents and correspondence in relation to the Diocese of Galway, Kilmacduagh and Kilfenora.

72   Galway Harbour Company

Address   New Docks
Galway

Telephone   (091) 562329/561874

Fax   (091) 563738

E-mail	galwayharbour@tinet.ie
Enquiries to	The C.E.O.
Opening hours and facilities	9.30–5.30, Mon–Fri; photocopying. National University of Ireland, Galway (q.v.) holds microfilm copies of Galway Harbour Commissioners records which may be consulted with written permission from Galway Harbour Company.

Major collections

Minute books, 1833–1997; arrivals and departures book, 1872–1901; tonnage and imports dues book 1884–1914; export dues book, 1882–1914; general maintenance and wages ledger, 1830–67; printed abstracts of accounts, 1854–1934.

73   Gamble Library

Address	Union Theological College of the Presbyterian Church in Ireland 108 Botanic Avenue Belfast BT7 1JT
Telephone	(01232) 205093
Fax	(01232) 316839
Enquiries to	The Librarian
Opening hours and facilities	9.00–5.00, Mon–Thur; 9.00–4.30, Fri; appointment necessary; photocopying

Major collections

Presbytery and Synod minutes of the Presbyterian Church in Ireland, 17th–19th century.

74   Garda Museum/Archives
Garda Síochána na hÉireann

Address	Record Tower Dublin Castle Dublin 2

Telephone	(01) 671 9597
Website address	www.geocities.com/CapitolHill/7900
Enquiries to	The Inspector in Charge
Opening hours and facilities	9.30–4.30, Mon–Sat; appointment advisable;

Major collections

The Museum displays historical material relating to the Royal Irish Constabulary, Dublin Metropolitan Police and An Garda Síochána, including uniforms, medals, photographs, certificates of merit and a small collection of private family letters.

The reading room contains R.I.C. directories, guides and codes of instruction [service records are available on microfilm in the National Archives (q.v)]; D.M.P. membership register, 1836–1925, and some personal records of membership, photographs, guides and codes of instruction and material relating to the early history of An Garda Síochána, as well as photographs and publications.

75   Genealogical Office

Address	2 Kildare Street Dublin 2
Telephone	(01) 603 0311
Fax	(01) 662 1062
Website address	www.heanet.ie/natlib/
Enquiries to	The Chief Herald/Deputy Chief Herald
Opening hours and facilities	10.00–12.30, 2.00–4.30, Mon–Fri; access to the collections may be had through the Manuscripts Reading Room of the National Library (q.v.), 10.00–8.30, Mon–Wed; 10.00–4.30, Thur–Fri; 10.00–12.30, Sat
Guides	Introductory leaflet

Major collections

Registers of arms, 16th century–.

Registrations of pedigrees, 16th century–.

Heraldic visitations, mainly of Counties Dublin and Wexford, 16th–17th century.
Sixteen volumes of funeral entries, 17th century.
Lords' Entry volumes (records relating to the introduction of peers to the Irish House of Lords), 18th century.
Records of the Order of St. Patrick (founded 1783).
Records of Sir William Beetham especially his abstracts from Irish prerogative wills (30 volumes) and pedigrees (23 volumes).
Commissioned genealogical searches, 19th–20th century.

76   General Register Office/ Oifig An Ard–Chláraitheora

Address	Joyce House 8/11 Lombard Street East Dublin 2
Telephone	(01) 635 0000/ 635 4430/ 635 4417
Fax	(01) 635 4440
E-mail	info@doh.ie
Enquiries to	Ard–Chláraitheoir Cúnta
Opening hours and facilities	9.30–12.30, 2.15–4.30, Mon–Fri; photocopying and certified copies of entries

Major collections
Registers of births registered in all Ireland, 1 Jan 1864–31 Dec 1921, and in Ireland (exclusive of the six north-eastern counties) from that date. Registers of deaths registered in all Ireland, 1 Jan 1864–31 Dec 1921, and in Ireland (exclusive of the six north-eastern counties) from that date. Registers of marriages in all Ireland, 1 Apr 1845–31 Dec 1863, except those celebrated by the Roman Catholic clergy.
Registers of all marriages registered in the whole of Ireland, 1 Jan 1864–1 Dec 1921, and in Ireland (exclusive of the six north-eastern counties) from that date.
Note: Only the indexes to the above records are open to public inspection, on payment of appropriate fee. Clients may purchase copies of individual entries identified in the Index.

77 General Register Office, Northern Ireland

Address   Oxford House
49/55 Chichester Street
Belfast BTI 4HL

Telephone   (01232) 252021/2/3/4

Fax   (01232) 252120

Website address www.nics.gov.uk/nisra/gro/

Enquiries to   The Deputy Registrar General

Opening hours 9.30–4.00, Mon–Fri; copying
and facilities

Guides   Information leaflets including *Records and search services*

Major collections

Records of births and deaths held in the General Register Office relate mainly to those registered since 1 Jan 1864 in that part of Ireland which is now Northern Ireland.

Marriage records are available in this office from 1922 only.

For information on a marriage which occurred subsequent to civil registration and prior to 1922 application should be made to the District Registrar, addresses of whom are obtainable from the General Register Office.

General searches are not undertaken by the office staff. The indexes are made available to the applicant or his appointed representative.

78 Geological Survey of Ireland

Address   Beggars Bush
Haddington Road
Dublin 4

Telephone   (01) 604 1420

Fax   (01) 668 1782

E-mail   LEONARDJ@tec.irlgov.ie

Website address	www.irlgov.ie/tec/gsi/
Enquiries to	The Public Office
Opening hours and facilities	Public Office 2.30–12.30; other times by appointment; photocopying

Major collections

Geological Survey of Ireland field sheets: original 6" to 1 mile (1:10, 560) geological field maps of the 26 counties, 1845–87 and early 20th century 6" glacial drift/land use maps of Cork, Dublin and Limerick city areas.

Geological Survey of Ireland archives: miscellaneous manuscripts from the Portlock Survey, 1820s–40s; Geological Survey of Ireland correspondence books, 1845–*c.*1900; du Noyer geological drawings, 1836–69; and printed material, including a reference set of geological maps of Ireland (largely 19th century) and pre-1900 geological books, from the Geological Survey library and the Portlock Bequest.

79   Geological Survey of Northern Ireland

Address	20 College Gardens Belfast BT9 6BS
Telephone	(01232) 666595
E-mail	gsni@bgs.ac.uk
Enquiries to	The Director
Opening hours and facilities	9.00–4.30, Mon–Fri; photocopying
Guides	*Regional Geology Guide to Northern Ireland*

Major collections

6" geological field maps of the 19th century Geological Survey of Ireland relating to Northern Ireland.

6" to 1 mile and 1:10,000 scale field maps of the Geological Survey of Northern Ireland, 1947–.

Library reference collection of maps, scientific papers, reports and records relating to the geology of Northern Ireland.

80   Glenstal Abbey

Address	Murroe County Limerick
Telephone	(061) 386103
Fax	(061) 386328
Enquiries to	The Archivist
Opening hours and facilities	Postal enquiry only

Major collections

Non–monastic: Carbery papers, 1658–1759; Sir Thomas Hackett papers, 1688–1720; Cloncurry papers, 1880–1909; correspondence between Mother Mary Martin and Bede Lebbe, 1930s; Fr John Sweetman papers, 1911–23; diaries of Richard Hobart, 1784–1802, Sir Thomas Kane, 1837, and J. Grene Barry, 1869–76; Gaelic League Ard-Craomh minute book, 1907–15.

Monastic: foundation correspondence; legal and administrative documents; financial, farm and school records; seniorate minute books, 1927–80; material relating to congresses, 1952–; material relating to the foundation in Nigeria, 1974–; private papers of deceased monks.

81   Company of Goldsmiths

Address	Goldsmiths Hall Assay Office Dublin Castle Dublin 2
Telephone	(01) 475 1286/478 0323;
Fax	(01) 478 3838
E-mail	assayirl@iol.ie
Enquiries to	The Assay Master
Opening hours and facilities	8.30–12.00, 2.00–4.00, Mon–Fri; by appointment

Guides	M. Clark & R. Refaussé (eds), *Directory of Historic Dublin Guilds* (Dublin, 1993)

Major collections

Archives of the Guild of All Saints (Goldsmiths) including: charter, 1637; minutes and work ledgers, 1637–; records of freemen, apprentices, brethren and members, 17th–19th century; accounts, 17th–20th century; letter books and certificates, 19th century.

The collection is available on microfilm in the National Library of Ireland.

82   Good Shepherd Sisters

Address	Pennywell Road Limerick
Telephone	(061) 415178
Fax	(061) 415147
Enquiries to	The Archivist
Opening hours and facilities	By appointment or postal enquiry; photocopying

Major collections

Papers relating to the general government of the congregation including the constitution and proceedings of general chapters and commissions; papers of successive superiors general and their councils;

Papers relating to the constitution and government of the province, 1862–, including proceedings of provincial chapters and inter-provincial meetings, 1869–; papers of provincial superiors and councils, 1869–; material relating to provincial policy and commissions; correspondence, accounts, statistics, annals and publications, 1870–.

Records of Limerick Convent, 1848–, including St Mary's Home, 1837–1976; St Joseph's Reformatory School, 1859–1972; St George's Industrial School, 1869–1970; group homes for children in care, hostels, shelters, and community service.

Records of convents, now closed, in New Ross, 1860–1967; Newry, 1944–84; Dunboyne, 1955–91

Photographs, press cuttings and reference material.

83   Guinness Ireland Archives

Address   St James' Gate
Dublin 8.

Telephone   (01) 453 6700 (ext. 45)

Enquiries to   The Archivist

Opening hours   9.30–5.30, Mon–Fri; by appointment only;
and facilities   photocopying

Major collections

Minute books of the Brewers' Guild of Dublin, 1759, Brewers' Corporation, 1805, and Coopers' Guild of Dublin, 1765–1836.

Charter of the Coopers' Guild granted by Charles II, 1666.

Account books of brewers' calculations, 1814–73; brewery memoranda, 1802–25, 1869–92; Board Orders, 1909–15; brewery statements and reports, 1883–99; Registry Department weekly notes, 1899–1922; Head Brewers' desk diaries, 1881–1933; Guiness guide books, 1888–1955; *Journal of the Institute of Brewing*, 1895–1982; brewery annual reports, 1899–1910; Board minutes, 1899–1930; Haine & Shand reports on overseas trade, 1904–25.

Correspondence with Lord Iveagh, 1921–7.

Ockham & Udiam Hop Farms annual reports, 1915–26.

Minutes and accounts of the British Association for the Advancement of Science, Dublin, 1956–8.

Minute books of Robert Perry & Sons Ltd, 1928–53.

84   Holy Faith Sisters
(Sisters of the Holy Faith)

Address   Holy Faith Convent
Glasnevin
Dublin 11

Telephone   (01) 837 3427

Enquiries to   The Archivist

Opening hours   By appointment; photocopying
and facilities

Major collections
Correspondence of founders, Margaret Aylward and Fr John Gowan CM, 1840s–. Life and lectures of Fr Gowan. Life and spiritual notes of John Joseph Steiner, a German convert and collector for St Brigid's Orphanage. Files relating to each convent of the Congregation including those in the Mission Fields. Aylward family papers. Personal effects of founders.

85   Holy Ghost Congregation (Irish Province)

Address	Temple Park Richmond Avenue South Dublin 6
Telephone	(01) 497 5127/497 7230
Fax	(01) 497 5399
E-mail	secretaryspiritan@tinet.ie
Enquiries to	The Archivist
Opening hours and facilities	By appointment; photocopying

Major collections
Material relating to the origins of the Congregation in Ireland; to its work at home including Blackrock College, Rockwell College, St Mary's College, Rathmines, St Michael's College, Ailesbury Road, Templeogue College, and Kimmage Manor Seminary and Institute; and on the foreign missions including Nigeria, Sierra Leone, The Gambia and Kenya.

86   Hugh Lane Municipal Gallery of Modern Art

Address	Charlemont House Parnell Square Dublin 1
Telephone	(01) 874 1903

Fax	(01) 872 2182
E-mail	hughlane@iol.ie
Website address	www.dublincorp.ie
Enquiries to	The Director
Opening hours	Access to archives by postal enquiry only

Major collections
Papers of Ellen Duncan, first Curator of the Gallery, 1914–22.
Archives of the Gallery, 1939–90.
Photographic collection, *c*.1907–90.
Papers of Harry Clarke (1889–1931), stained glass artist.

87   Incorporated Law Society of Ireland

Address	Blackhall Place Dublin 7
Telephone	(01) 672 4800
Fax	(01) 672 4845
E-mail	general@lawsociety.ie
Website address	www.lawsociety.ie
Enquiries to	The Librarian
Opening hours and facilities	8.30–5.30, Mon–Fri; by appointment; photocopying

Major collections
Minute books of meetings of Council, 1922–.

88   Infant Jesus Sisters – Nicolas Barré

Address	56 St Lawrence Road Clontarf Dublin 3
Telephone	(01) 833 9577
Fax	(01) 853 0857

Enquiries to   The Archivist

Opening hours   Postal enquiry only; photocopying
and facilities

Major collections
Material relating to the history of the Infant Jesus Sisters in Ireland and
England, 1892–; to the educational Apostolate of the Irish Sisters in
Malaysia, Singapore, Japan, Australia, Nigeria, Cameroons and Peru;
to the Founder, Venerable Nicholas Barré, and to the general history of
the Institute, 1662–. Includes correspondence, photographs, reports of
meetings and councils, and account books from the farm, brush factories, sawmills and knitting factories set up in Ireland in the early 20th
century to combat emigration.

89   Institution of Engineers of Ireland

Address   22 Clyde Road
Ballsbridge
Dublin 4

Telephone   (01) 668 4341

Fax   (01) 668 5508

E-mail   iei@iol.ie

Enquiries to   The Librarian

Opening hours   9.00–5.00, Mon–Fri; photocopying
and facilities

Guides   N. Hughes, *Index to the Transactions of the Institution
of Engineers of Ireland, 1845–1991* (Dublin, 1992)

Major collections
Transactions of the Institution of Engineers of Ireland, 1845–1991.
Correspondence and reports of the eminent railway engineer John
MacNeill, 1826–44.

90   The Irish Agricultural Museum

Address   Johnstown Castle
                   Old Farmyard
                   Wexford

Telephone   (053) 42888

Fax   (053) 42213

E-mail   AOSULLIVAN@johnstown.teagasc.ie

Enquiries to   The Curator

Opening hours   By appointment; photocopying
and facilities

Major collections

Small amount of mill account books and estate records, mostly from
County Wexford, *c.*1850–1900. Malting industry records for Wexford
and Castlebridge.
Machinery manufacturers' catalogues, 1900–50.

91   Irish Architectural Archive

Address   73 Merrion Square
                   Dublin 2
                   from January 2000
                   44/45 Merrion Square
                   Dublin 2

Telephone   (01) 676 3430

Fax   (01) 676 6309

E-mail   iaa1@iaa.iol.ie

Website address www.archeire.com/iaa

Enquiries to   The Archive Administrator or Archive Director

Opening hours   10.00–1.00, 2.30–5.00, Tue–Fri;
and facilities   photocopying; photography

Major collections

The Irish Architectural Archive collects, preserves and makes available
records of every type relating to the architecture of Ireland. The holdings
comprise in excess of 100,000 architectural drawings, 300,000 pho-

tographs, 12,000 printed items and several dozen architectural models, 1690s–1990s. The collections include information on every notable Irish architect, on every important Irish building period or style, and on most significant buildings in Ireland.

Major collections include: Ashlin & Coleman; Boyd Barrett Murphy O'Connor; Burgage; Rudolph Maximillian Butler; Charleville Forest; Cullen & Company; C.P. Curran; Dublin Artisans Dwellings Company; Emo Court; Desmond FitzGerald; Charles Geoghan; Guinness Drawings; Alan Hope; Brendan Jeffers; Alfred Jones Biographical Index; McCurdy & Mitchell; Raymond McGrath; Munden & Purcell; Donal O'Neill Flanagan; Patterson Kempster Shortall; Anthony Reddy Associates; Fred Rogerson; R.I.A.I. Murray Collection; Royal (Collins) Barracks; Royal Institute of the Architects of Ireland Archives; Robinson Keefe & Devane; Scott Tallon Walker; Michael Scott; Sibthorpe; Stephenson Gibney; Townley Hall; Tyndall Hogan Hurley; Workhouse Collection.

Photographic collections include Automobile Association Photographs; B.K.S. Aerial Photographs; Buildings of Ireland Photographs; Alec R. Day A.R.P.S. Collection; J.V. Downes Slide Collection; Kieran Glendining Collection; Green Studio Collection; Thomas Gunn Collection; Westropp Albums; as well as on-going photographic survey work carried out by the I.A.A.

92   Irish Capuchin Archives

Address	Capuchin Friary Church Street Dublin 7
Telephone	(056) 21439
Fax	(056) 22025
Enquiries to	The Archivist Capuchin Friary Friart Street Kilkenny
Opening hours and facilities	By postal or telephone enquiry only

Major collections

Administrative documents and correspondence of the Irish Province, 1885–1970.

Material relating to the history of the Irish Province, 1633–.

93 Irish Christian Brothers (Northern – St Mary's – Province)

Address	Christian Brothers' Provincialate 274 North Circular Road Dublin 7
Telephone	(01) 868 0247
Fax	(01) 838 1075
E-mail	cbprov@tinet.ie
Enquiries to	The Archivist or Revd Brother Provincial
Opening hours and facilities	Postal enquiry; photocopying

Major collections

Material relating to the history, evolution and administration of the Congregation. Material relating to St Mary's Province, 1956–.

94 Irish Christian Brothers St Helen's Provincialate

Address	York Road Dún Laoghaire County Dublin
Telephone	(01) 280 1214/284 1656
Fax	(01) 284 1657
Enquiries to	The Archivist
Opening hours	10.00–3.30, Mon–Fri, excluding Holy days; appointment necessary

Major collections

Annals of Christian Brothers' discontinued establishments from throughout the country. Minutes of Provincial Chapters. Registers of postulants, novices and industrial schools. Minutes of the Christian Brothers' Education Committee.

Material relating to the life and work of Br Edmund Ignatius Rice and the early brothers.

Collection of historical and educational publications including Christian
Brothers' publications; Reports of the Commissioners of Inquiry into
Irish Education (1827); and correspondence concerning the Erasmus
Smith Schools Act Scheme, 1941.

95   Irish Film Archive
Film Institute of Ireland

Address	6 Eustace Street Dublin 2
Telephone	(01) 679 5744
Fax	(01) 677 8755
E-mail	archive@ifc.ie (film, tape and paper archives) info@ifc.ie (library)
Enquiries to	The Archive Curator (film and tape) The Librarian (library and paper archives)
Opening hours and facilities	film and tape: 10.00–1.00, 2.00–5.00, Mon–Fri; appointment necessary; scale of charges on application; paper archives: 10.00–1.00, Mon–Fri; appointment necessary; reference library: 2.00–5.30, Mon–Fri, 2.00–7.00 Wed; no appointment necessary; photocopying

Major collections

The film collection numbers over 15,000 cans, acquired by donation from
public and private bodies, reflecting the history of professional and amateur film production in Ireland from 1897.

Much of the film collection has been transferred to videotape for reference
purposes, the tape collection now anounting to over 1,000 VHS tapes of
Irish material.

The paper archives collection includes stills, posters and other documents
relating to Irish cinema.

The Tiernan McBride Library contains over 1,200 books, film periodicals and film-related CD ROMs on all aspects of national and international cinema. A cuttings file on Irish film production is also main-
tained.

96   Irish Jesuit Archives

Address	35 Lower Leeson Street Dublin 2
Telephone	(01) 676 1248
Fax	(01) 676 2984
Enquiries to	The Archivist/Assistant Archivist
Opening hours and facilities	By appointment
Guides	Fergus O'Donoghue SJ, 'Irish Jesuit Archives', *Archivium Hibernicum* xli (1986), 64–71. Stephen Redmond SJ, 'A Guide to the Irish Jesuit Province Archives', *Archivium Hibernicum* l (1996), 127–131

Major collections
Administrative and pastoral material, including correspondence with the Jesuit generalate; papers of noted Jesuits; papers relating to property; manuscripts of books and sermons; retreat notes; manuscripts in Irish; photographs; papers relating to Irish Jesuit missions in Australia, the Far East and Zambia. Original manuscripts cover the period 1575–1970, transcripts 1540–1774.

97   Irish Jewish Museum

Address	3/4 Walworth Road South Circular Road Dublin 8
Telephone	(01) 453 1797/676 0737
Enquiries to	The Curator
Opening hours and facilities	11.00–3.30, Sun, Tue, Thur, May–Sept; 10.30–2.30, Sun only, Oct–Apr; other times by appointment

Major collections
Minute books and records of various communal institutions and synagogues, registers of births, marriages and deaths, correspondence and communal publications, 1820–.

98   Irish Labour History Society Museum and Archives

Address	Beggar's Bush
	Haddington Road
	Dublin 4
Telephone	(01) 668 1071
Fax	(01) 668 1071
Enquiries to	The Supervisor
Opening hours and facilities	10.00–1.00, 2.00–4.30, Mon–Fri
Guides	Summary descriptions of collections acquired by the ILHS and deposited in University College Dublin Archives Department (q.v.) or held in the ILHS Museum and Archives are published in *Saothar*, the Society's journal, 5–16 (1979–91); the journal also includes guides to collections of labour interest in other repositories, both in Ireland and abroad.

Major collections

Postal and Telecommunications Workers' Union (merged with the Communications Union of Ireland in 1989 to form the Communication Workers' Union): rule books and annual conference reports; branch records; material relating to the Union's involvement with ITUC/ICTU, the Labour Party and international bodies; publications of other postal workers' unions.

Papers of William Norton (1900–63) relating to all aspects of Norton's public life as general secretary of the POWU, Labour Party TD for Kildare, 1932–62, leader of the Labour Party, 1932–60, Tánaiste and Minister for Social Welfare, 1948–52, and Minister for Industry and Commerce, 1954–7.

Irish Women Workers' Union: minute books and annual reports; records relating to the union's representation of laundry and print workers and its participation in the national trade union movement and the Labour Party, 1917–84.

Workers' Union of Ireland records, 1924–89: includes administrative and branch records, mainly late 1940s–, and including some papers of James Larkin Jnr.

Association of Secondary Teachers of Ireland: organisational and branch records including material on educational policy, 1919–94.

Some private paper collections including papers of Cathal O'Shannon.

99   Irish Land Commission, Records Branch

Address	National Archives Building Bishop Street Dublin 8
Telephone	(01) 475 0766
Fax	(01) 478 5857
Enquiries to	The Keeper of Records
Opening hours and facilities	10.00–12.30, 2.30–4.30, Mon–Fri; by appointment only. Limited access and photocopying in accordance with Land Commission Rules

Major collections

The largest series of records held by the Land Commission Records Branch are the title documents and ancillary papers pertaining to estates acquired by both the Land Commission and the Congested Districts Board under different Land Acts since 1881. As well as deeds dating from the 17th century these include abstracts of title, maps lodged by vendors of estates, schedules of particulars of tenancies, orders vesting estates in the Land Commission, schedules of particulars of the allocation of the estate purchase moneys, tenants' fiated purchase agreements and resale maps. Other record series created under the auspices of the numerous administrative branches of the Land Commission include the following: Irish Land Commission Minute Books, 1892–1918; Fair Rent Orders and Agreements, 1881–1920; Apportionment Orders, Right of Way Orders and other Orders of the Judicial Commissioners, 1881–; Registers of Affidavits, 1881–1974; Secretariat files, 1881–1985; Originating Statements by Landlords, 1892–1904; Final Schedules of Incumbrances, 1886–1951; Land Purchase Department Records of Proceedings [1885–1955]. Records of the Church Temporalities Commission includes leases of Church property, *c.*1600–1869; mortgages, conveyances and grants in perpetuity, 1869–*c.*1880; records relating to Tithe Rent Charge, 1869–1973; Commutation Claims, 1870–2; Applotment Books, 1872; Investigators' Reports, 1869–79; Seal Books, 1908–27; glebe maps, 1835–77.

100   Irish Linen Centre & Lisburn Museum

Address	Market Square Lisburn BT28 1AG
Telephone	(01846) 663377
Fax	(01846) 672624
Enquiries to	The Research Officer
Opening hours and facilities	9.30–5.00, Mon–Fri; appointment preferred; photocopying; photography; microfilm reader/printer

Major collections

The library and archives of the former Lambeg Industrial Research Association (LIRA) includes books, journals, pamphlets and ephemera, 18th–20th centuries; together with the administrative records of the organisation from its foundation in the 1920s until its closure in 1993.
Manuscript material and maps relating to Lisburn.
Photographic collection.

101   Irish Railway Record Society

Address	Heuston Station Dublin 8
Telephone	(01238) 528428
Enquiries to	The Archivist
Opening hours and facilities	8.00–10.00, Tue; by appointment
Guides	Joseph Leckey, *The Records of the Irish Transport Genealogical Archive*. Occasional Publication No. 7 of the Irish Railway Record Society (Belfast, 1985); Joseph Leckey and Peter Rigney, *IRRS Archival Collections D1–D10* (Dublin, 1976); Joseph Leckey, *The Records of the County Donegal Railways* (Belfast, 1980)

Major collections

Transport archives, 18th century–, including waterways, roads, and air transport, but predominantly railways. Private collections and non-current archives of CIÉ, the national transport undertaking, and its constituent companies.

Incorporates Irish Transport Genealogical Archive: the personal records of transport employees, 1870s–1950s as far as these have been located. Fine collection of transport and other directories.

Ordnance Survey maps covering much of the railway system, with 5,000 other maps and drawings.

Most complete collection of parliamentary plans of Irish railways outside the House of Lords Record Office. Other books of plans include docks, drainage, tramways, reservoirs, markets, and hotels as well as contractors' plans of railways.

102   Irish Rugby Football Union

Address   62 Lansdowne Road
Dublin 4

Telephone   (01) 668 4601

Fax   (01) 660 5640

Website address   www.irfu.ie

Enquiries to   The Secretary

Opening hours and facilities   By appointment; photocopying

Major collections

Minute books, miscellaneous papers, photographs, press cuttings, memorabilia, 1874–.

103   Irish Theatre Archive

Address   c/o City Assembly House
58 South William Street
Dublin 2

Telephone   (01) 677 5877

Fax   (01) 677 5954

Enquiries to   The Honorary Archivist

Opening hours and facilities   10.00–1.00, 2.00–5.00, Mon–Fri, by appointment; photocopying; photography;

Major collections

Archives of major theatres including An Damer; Cork Theatre Company; Charabanc Theatre Company; Dublin Theatre Festival; Gaiety Theatre, Dublin; Irish Theatre Company; and the Brendan Smith Academy.

Private papers of players and designers including Eddie Cooke; Ursula Doyle; Donald Finlay; James N. Healy; Eddie Johnston; Nora Lever; Dennis Noble; Jimmy O'Dea; Shelah Richards; and Cecil Sheridan.

Extensive collection of programmes, posters, photographs, press cuttings, prompt-books, costume and stage designs relating to theatres, amateur groups and theatre clubs; together with original plays in typescript and manuscript.

104 Irish Traditional Music Archive/ Taisce Cheol Dúchais Éireann

Address	63 Merrion Square
	Dublin 2
Telephone	(01) 661 9699
Fax	(01) 662 4585
Website address	www.itma.ie
Enquiries to	The Secretary
Opening hours and facilities	10.00–1.00, 2.0–5.00, Mon–Fri; photocopying; photography
Guides	Nicholas Carolan, *Irish Traditional Music Archive/ Taisce Cheol Dúchais Éireann: The First Ten Years/ Na Chéad Deich mBliana (1997)*; Hugh Shields, *Tunes of the Munster Pipers. Irish Traditional Music from the James Goodman* Collections, vol. 1 (1998); Colette Moloney, *The Irish Music Manuscripts of Edward Bunting (1773–1843): an introduction and* catalogue (1999); information leaflet available on request

Major collections

Over 10,000 hours of sound recordings, 1890s–: commercial 78s, SPs, EPs, LPs, audio cassettes and CDs. Field sound recordings on cylinders, reel-to-reel tapes, audio cassettes, DAT, mini discs and CDs, include the Breathnach, Shields, Hamilton, Ó Conluain, Carroll-Mackenzie, MacWeeney, de Buitléar, R.T.É. and B.B.C. Radio collections, 20th century.

Printed matter: works of reference, serials, song and instrumental collections, studies, sheet music, ballad sheets and ephemera including posters, flyers and newspaper cuttings, 18th century–.

More than 3,000 photographic and other images, 19th century–.

Music manuscripts, theses and other unpublished material, 18th century–.

Over 500 video recordings, 20th century–.

105   Jesus and Mary Sisters (Congregation of the Religious of Jesus and Mary)

Address	Convent of Jesus and Mary Our Lady's Grove Goatstown Road Dublin 14
Telephone	(01) 298 4569
Fax	(01) 296 3793
Enquiries to	The Archivist
Opening hours and facilities	By appointment; photocopying

Major collections

Archives of the congregation in the Irish Province including correspondence with higher superiors and material relating to the ministry of Irish Sisters in other provinces of the congregation.

106   James Joyce Museum

Address	Joyce Tower Sandycove County Dublin
Telephone	(01) 280 9265/
Fax	(01) 280 9265
Enquiries to	The Curator

Opening hours and facilities	10.00–1.00, 2.00–5.00, Mon–Sat, 2.00–6.00, Sun. and public holidays, Apr–Oct; by arrangement, Nov–Mar, contact the Dublin Writers' Museum (q.v.)

Major collections
Letters and papers, portraits, photographs, first and rare editions, printed ephemera and personal possessions of James Joyce (1882–1941), including his death mask, guitar, waistcoat and cabin trunk.

107 The John F. Kennedy Arboretum Dúchas The Heritage Service

Address	New Ross County Wexford
Telephone	(051) 388171
Fax	(051) 388171
Enquiries to	The Director
Opening hours and facilities	10.00–8.00, May–Aug; 10.00–6.30, Apr, Sept; 10.00–5.00, Oct–Mar

Major collections
Records for each specimen in the arboretum, which contains 4,500 species, including height, stem diameter and crown spread, 1968–1989.
Records of species in 200 forest plots including height, basal area and volume, 1966–1995.

108 Kerry County Library

Address	Moyderwell Tralee County Kerry
Telephone	(066) 21200
Fax	(066) 29202
E-mail	libraryt@hotmail.com
Enquiries to	The County Librarian
Opening hours and facilities	10.30–5.00, Mon–Sat; photocopying

Major collections
Board of Guardian records.

Minute books: Cahirciveen, 1905–22; Dingle, 1840–1920; Glin 1870–91; Kenmare, 1840–1921; Killarney, 1840–1923; Listowel, 1845–1922; Tralee 1845–1922.

Rough minute books: Dingle, 1849–1921; Killarney, 1840–71; Listowel, 1856–99; Tralee, 1845–1922.

Rural District Council minute books: Caherciveen, 1900–25; Dingle, 1899–1925; Kenmare, 1899–1921; Killarney, 1900–25; Listowel, 1901–11; Tralee 1900–25.

Kerry Board of Health minute books: Board of Health & Public Assistance, 1930–42; Board of Health, 1925–31; Board of Health and Labourers' Acts, 1937–42; Board of Health Tuberculosis Section, 1927–31; Board of Health and Public Assistance Tuberculosis Section, 1932–42.

109   Kerry Diocesan Archives

Address	Bishop's House
	Killarney
	County Kerry
Telephone	(064) 31168
Fax	(064) 31364
Enquiries to	The Archivist
Opening hours and facilities	By appointment

Major collections
Material connected with episcopates of Nicholas Madgett, Bishop of Kerry (1753–74) and of each subsequent bishop of the diocese, as well as more personal papers of several bishops and some priests.

110   Kildare County Library Local History Department

Address	Athgarvan Road
	Newbridge
	County Kildare
Telephone	(045) 431109

Fax	(045) 432490
Enquiries to	The Librarian, Local History Department
Opening hours and facilities	By appointment; photocopying

Major collections

Board of Guardians minute books: Naas, 1841–1922; Athy, 1914–20; Celbridge, 1910–19.

Minute books of Kildare County Council, 1899–1966.

Grand Jury presentments, 1810–93.

Rural District Council minute books: Celbridge, 1907–13; Edenderry, 1899–1919; Naas 1903–21.

Shackleton collection: letters, poems and books relating to the Shackleton family of Ballitore, late 18th–early 19th century.

Teresa Brayton collection: poems, short stories, letters, photographs and memorabilia relating to Teresa Brayton, author of *The Old Bog Road*, 1868–1943.

111 Kildare & Leighlin Diocesan Archives

Address	Bishop's House
	Carlow
Telephone	(0503) 31102
Fax	(0503) 32478
Enquiries to	The Diocesan Chancellor
Opening hours and facilities	By arrangement with the Diocesan Chancellor; application in writing

Major collections

Papers of bishops, 1745–1930. Some collections relating to clergy. Parish returns and vicars' visitation papers. Accounts, notebooks, and sermon manuscripts.

112 Kilkenny Archaeological Society

Address	Rothe House
	Kilkenny
Telephone	(056) 22893

Fax	(056) 51108
Enquiries to	The Librarian
Opening hours and facilities	2.30–4.30, 7.30–9.30, Tue; 2.30–4.30, Wed; at other times by arrangement

Major collections

Langrishe Papers, Knocktopher Abbey, County Kilkenny, 1667–1923: estate records, family correspondence, wills, maps, surveys, rent records and leases.

Buggy & Co., solicitors, Kilkenny: legal papers relating to numerous Kilkenny families, *c.*1823–1940.

Collections of legal documents including wills, probate records, marriage settlements, leases, mortgages, affidavits, and correspondence, including some papers of Wheeler–Cuffe, Lyrath, Kilkenny, and Mrs Montague, Kilferagh, *c.*1706–1945.

Local newspaper reference collection, 18th–20th centuries.

Research files on various notable local families including the Rothes, Langtons, Andersons and Crottys. Register of Kilkenny World War 1 combatants.

113   Kilkenny Corporation

Address	City Hall High Street Kilkenny
Telephone	(056) 21076
Fax	(056) 63422
Enquiries to	The Town Clerk
Opening hours and facilities	By appointment or postal enquiry; photocopying

Major collections

Charters, Grants, Letters Patent of the City of Kilkenny, 1170–1862, including the 1st Charter of Wiliam Earl of Pembroke to the Burgesses of Kilkenny, 1170, and the Charter of James I, 1609, creating Kilkenny a city. Minute books of the Corporation, including the first minute book, the 'Liber Primus Kilkennienses', 1231–1538; minutes of the 'Mayor and Citizens' of Kilkenny, 1656–1843; minutes of the 'Mayor Aldermen and Burgesses', 1843–1952; minutes of various committee meetings, 1892–1938; proceedings of the Corporation of Irishtown, 1544–1834; minutes of the Kilkenny Urban Sanitary Authority, 1875–6, 1917–42. Grand Roll of Freeman of the city of Kilkenny, 1760–. Deeds, conveyances, leases, letters, petitions and addresses, *c.*13th–19th century.

114   Kilkenny County Library

Address	6 John's Quay Kilkenny
Telephone	(056) 22021/22606
Fax	(056) 70233
E-mail	katlibs@iol.ie
Enquiries to	The Assistant Librarian
Opening hours and facilities	10.30–1.00,2.00–5.00, Mon–Fri; 7.00–9.00, Tue & Wed evenings; 10.30–1.30, Sat; photocopying

Major collections

Local administrative records including Board of Guardian records, 1839–1923; Rural District Council records, 1894–1926; Grand Jury records, 1838–98; Registers of Electors, 1896–1994.

Records of Kilkenny County Council including Committee of Agriculture, 1924–41, County Board of Health, 1922–42, County Library Committee, 1910–, County Council minute books, 1899–1990, County Manager's orders, 1942–, valuation lists, rent and rate books and general files from various Council departments.

Callan Corporation indentures, 1720–1819, and Callan Town Commissioners administrative records, 1897–1944.

Private collections include indentures, wills and mortages, 1760–1924; Kilkenny City business records, early 20th century; records of Theatre Unlimited in Kilkenny, 1985–6; Arts Week records, 1974–86; and business records of Clover Meats, Waterford, 1920–80.

Photographic collections including the Lawrence, Valentine, and Seymore Crawford collections; Bolton Street College of Technology Architectural Faculty amenity study photographs, 1970; Bord Fáilte collection; industrial archaeology survey of County Kilkenny; and various collections of photographs of locations and activities in the city and county, early 20th century.

115   Killaloe Diocesan Archives

Address   Westbourne
                          Ennis
                          County Clare

Telephone   (065) 682 8638

Fax   (065) 684 2538

E-mail   cildalus@iol.ie

Enquiries to   The Diocesan Secretary

Opening hours By appointment or postal enquiry;
and facilities   photocopying

Major collections

Notebooks of Canon John Clancy: mainly extracts from 19th century newspapers.

Parish notes: files for each parish consisting mainly of returns to a questionnaire relating to antiquities, folklore and churches, prepared by Dermot F. Gleeson in the early 1940s.

Material on microfilm relating to Killaloe from the Congregation de Propaganda Fide in Rome, 1620–1900.

Notebooks, manuscripts and books of Monsignor Ignatius Murphy.

116   Kilmainham Gaol Museum

Address   Inchicore
                          Dublin 8

Telephone   (01) 453 5984

Fax   (01) 453 2037

Enquiries to   The Curator

Opening hours 2.00–6.00, Wed & Sun, Oct–May; 11.00–6.00,
and facilities   June–Sept; otherwise by appointment;
                          photocopying; photography

Major collections

A miscellaneous collection of documents, photographs, uniforms, arms and personal effects, 1798–1924, with particularly interesting material from the 1916–22 period.

117   Kilmore Diocesan Archives

Address   Bishops's House
Cullies
Cavan

Telephone   (049) 431496

Enquiries to   The Diocesan Archivist

Opening hours   By appointment
and facilities

Major collections

Correspondence and papers of bishops including Lenten pastorals, letters to Rome, private office papers, sermons, visitation books, deeds, plans, wills, photographs and press cuttings, 1836–.

Correspondence and papers of priests of the diocese including the collections of Owen F. Traynor, T.P. Cunningham and Dr Philip O'Connell, the diocesan historian.

118   Kilrush Urban District Council and Kilrush (Cappa Pier) Harbour Authority

Address   Town Hall
Kilrush
County Clare

Telephone   (065) 51047/51596

Fax   (065) 52821

Enquiries to   The Town Clerk

Opening hours   9.30–5.00, Mon–Fri; photocopying
and facilities

Major collections

Minute books, 1885–; harbour arrivals and departures books, 1875–; general maintenance and wages ledgers and printed abstracts of accounts, 1885–.

119   The King's Hospital

Address	Palmerstown Dublin 20
Telephone	(01) 626 5933
Fax	(01) 623 0349
E-mail	kingshos@iol.ie
Enquiries to	The Archivist
Opening hours and facilities	By appointment
Guides	Brief listing in Lesley Whiteside, A *History of the King's Hospital, Dublin* (2nd ed., Dublin, 1985)

Major collections

Records relating to the school: annual accounts, 1669–1976, 1771–1809, 1858–; building accounts, 1669–75, 1742–45; partial accounts for the building of Blackhall Place, 1773–4; board minutes, 1674–1746, 1779–1829, 1841–; general committee minutes, 1798–1823, 1829–; headmasters' reports, 1884–; lists of pupils, some incomplete, 1675–1867, 1895–; memorials for admission, 1890–1940; fee registers, 1908; reminiscences of past pupils; records relating to the sporting history of the school, 1890–, including a large collection of photographs.

Records relating to property: rentals and rent ledgers, 1669–83, 1730–79, 1794–; maps of estates in Dublin and Tipperary; deeds.

Records of Mercer's School, Castleknock, County Dublin: Board minutes, 1832–1968; accounts and rent rolls, 1738–1822; accounts, 1864–1901; lists of pupils, 1865–; deeds of property in Dublin; small collection of photographs.

Records of Morgan's School, Castleknock, County Dublin: Board minutes, 1909–58; takeover papers; deeds.

Oral history collection of past pupils and staff; small collection of videos.

120   King's Inns
(The Honorable Society of King's Inns)

Address	Henrietta Street Dublin 1

Telephone	(01) 878 2119
E-mail	library@kingsinns.ie
Website address	www.iol.ie/kingsinns
Enquiries to	The Librarian
Opening hours and facilities	10.00–8.30, Mon–Thur; 10.30–6.00, Fri; I 0.00–1.00, Sat; outside academic year Library opens 10.00–5.00, Mon–Fri; researchers should write in advance stating the nature of their enquiry; photocopying
Guides	Julitta Clancy, *Records of the Honourable Society of King's Inns: guide and descriptive lists* (in–house production, 1989); Nigel Cochrane, 'The archives and manuscripts of the King's Inns Library', *Irish Archives* 1 (1989), 25–30; Pádraig de Brún, *Catalogue of Irish Manuscripts in King's Inns Library Dublin* (Dublin Institute for Advanced Studies, 1972); Edward Keane, P. Beryl Phair and Thomas U. Sadleir (eds), *King's Inns Admission Papers, 1607–1867* (Dublin, Irish Manuscripts Commission, 1982); Colum Kenny, 'The records of King's Inns, Dublin', in Daire Hogan and W.N. Osborough (eds), *Brehons, Serjeants and Attorneys* (Dublin, Irish Academic Press & Irish Legal History Society, 1990), 231–48; T. Power, 'The "Black Book" of King's Inn: an introduction with an abstract of contents', *The Irish Jurist* xx (1985), 135–312; Wanda Ryan-Smolin, *King's Inns Portraits* (Dublin, The Council of King's Inns, 1992).

Major collections

Archives of the Society, 1607–1917, which include the 'Black Book' 1607–1730, Bench Minutes, 1792–1917, admission records of barristers and admission records of attorneys up to 1866.

29 Irish language manuscripts, the majority dating from the 18th century, but five of which were written as early as the 15th century.

Private paper collection of John Patrick Prendergast (1808–1893).

Manuscripts of Bartholomew Thomas Duhigg (*c*.1750–1813), Assistant Librarian to the Society.

Manuscript parliamentary journals and miscellaneous legal manuscripts.

121   Kinsale Harbour Commissioners

Address   Harbour Office
                       Custom's Quay
                       Kinsale
                       County Cork

Telephone   (021) 772503

Fax   (021) 774695

Enquiries to   The Harbour Master

Opening hours   By appointment
and facilities

Major collections
Minute books, 1870–; arrivals and departures books, 1898–; export and
    import books, 1898–; maps, plans and drawings of the harbour, 1883;
    cash books, 1879–; bye-laws, 1870–

122   The Labour Party

Address   17 Ely Place
                       Dublin 2

Telephone   (01) 661 2615

Fax   (01) 661 2640

E-mail   ray_kavanagh@labour.ie

Website address   www.labour.ie

Enquiries to   General Secretary

Opening hours   9.30–4.30, Mon–Fri; photocopying
and facilities

Major collections
Records of the parliamentary party, 1970–; records of the party adminis-
    tration, 1970s–
Annual reports, 1912–.

123   Land Registry

Address	Central Office Chancery Street Dublin 7
Telephone	(01) 670 7500
Fax	(01) 804 8074
E-mail	leahyf@landreg.irlgov.ie
Website address	www.irlgov.ie/landreg/
Enquiries to	The Chief Executive/Registrar of Deeds and Titles
Opening hours and facilities	10.30–4.30, Mon–Fri; photocopying; microfilming, digitising
Guides	*Land Registry and Registry of Deeds Information Guide* (1998)

Major collections

Folio Series: each folio contains a description of a particular holding, the name, address and description of the owner and details of any burden or charges affecting the property, 1892–.

Land Registry Maps: each map contains plans drawn of each holding indicating the position and boundaries of the property the ownership of which has been registered, 1892–.

124   Laois County Library

Address	County Hall Portlaoise
Telephone	(0502) 22044
Fax	(0502) 22313
Enquiries to	The County Librarian
Opening hours and facilities	9.00–5.00, Mon–Fri; by appointment; photocopying

Major collections

Boards of Guardians minute books: Abbeyleix Union, 1844–1919; Mountmellick Union, 1845–1920; Donaghmore Union, 1851–86.

Dureen Dispensary minute book, 1880–98.

Grand Jury presentment book, Stradbally summer assizes, 1816–42.

Urban District Council minute books: Abbeyleix, 1909–25; Athy, 1913–25; Cloneygowan, 1903–23; Mountmellick, 1899–1926; Roscrea, 1905–17; Slievemargy, 1909–25.

Laois County Council: Queen's County minute book, 1900–25; rate books, 1916–62; account books, 1927–37; Barrow drainage scheme rate books, 1939–46; blind welfare scheme, 1934–52; free milk distribution scheme, 1942–50; tuberculosis committee minute books, 1915–25; road works, 1929–30; minute book and correspondence of Portlaoise swimming pool, 1967–76.

Hospital records: register of cases sent to external hospitals, 1926–58; home assistance, 1934–53; hospital administration records for County Infirmary, 1880–1924; County Hospital, 1933–60; County Home, 1933–4; Abbeyleix District Hospital, 1924–53; St Brigid's Sanitorium, Shaen, 1930–61.

Board of Health records, 1907–60; Public Assistance minute books, 1924–40.

Bye–laws of Maryborough, 1731; tenants' account book, Deerpark, Kilkenny, 1836–46; Stradbally Petty Sessions order books, 1851–96; Trustees of River Nore Drainage minute book, 1855–1939, and account books, 1855–1945; Maryborough Lawn Tennis & Croquet Club minute book, 1914–31.

125   Ledwidge Museum

Address

Jeanville
Slane
County Meath

Telephone

(041) 24244/24544/2467

Enquiries to

The Secretary
Ledwidge Museum
14 Ledwidge Terrace
Slane
County Meath

Opening hours and facilities

10.00–1.00, 2.00–6.00, Sun–Sat, summer;
10.00–1.00, 2.00–4.30, Sun–Sat, winter

Guides

General information leaflet

Major collections
Manuscript poems, correspondence and memorabilia of the poet Frances
  Ledwidge, 1887–1917.

126 Leitrim County Library

Address	Ballinamore County Leitrim
Telephone	(078) 44012
Fax	(078) 44425
Enquiries to	Leabharlannaí Contae
Opening hours and facilities	10.00–1.00, 2.00–5.00, Mon–Fri; photocopying

Major collections
Mohill Board of Guardians minute books, 1839–1922; Manorhamilton
  Board of Guardians minute books, 1839–1923; Carrick–on–Shannon
  Board of Guardians minute books, 1843–1919.
Records of Kinlough Rural District Council, 1902–25; Mohill Rural
  District Council, 1899–1924; Manorhamilton Rural District Council,
  1899–1925.
Estate papers from some Leitrim estates.
Large collection of ledgers and account books from various shops and
  business premises.
Minute books of various committees.

127 Limerick Diocesan Archives

Address	Diocesan Office 6 O'Connell Street Limerick
Telephone	(061) 315856
Fax	(061) 310186
E-mail	diocoff@tinet.ie
Website address	www.limerick-diocese.org
Enquiries to	The Diocesan Secretary

| Opening hours and facilities | Permission must be sought to consult diocesan archives available on microfilm in the National Library of Ireland (q.v.) |

Major collections

Records on microfilm in the National Library include baptismal and marriage records of the parishes of the diocese to 1900.

Material held in the diocesan archives includes the 14th century Black Book of Limerick.

128 Limerick Museum

| Address | 1 John's Square North
Limerick
from mid-1999
Castle Lane
Nicholas Street
Limerick |
Telephone	(061) 417826
Enquiries to	The Curator
Opening hours and facilities	10.00–1.00, 2.15–5.00, Tue–Sat; Curator available Mon–Fri, by appointment; photocopying; photography

Major collections

Miscellaneous documents, maps and photographs relating to Limerick, *c.*17th century–.

129 Limerick Regional Archives

| Address | The Granary
Michael Street
Limerick |
Telephone	(061) 410777
Fax	(061) 415125
Enquiries to	The Regional Archivist
Opening hours and facilities	9.30–1.00, 2.15–5.30, Mon–Fri; prior notice advisable as records are held at various locations; fee-paid research service available; photocopying; microfilming

Major collections

Poor Law minute books, 1838–1923 and Rural District Council minute books, 1899–1925 for Counties Limerick, Clare and Tipperary.

Limerick County Council minute books, 1898–; County Board of Health minute books, 1923–44.

Limerick Corporation: Freedom records, 1737–1905; Council and Committee minute books: 1841 –; Tholsel Court records, 1773–1833.

Commissioners for St Michael's parish: minute books, 1819–44; rate books, 1811–44; night watch reports, 1833–49.

Limerick Chamber of Commerce: minute books, 1807–; export books, 1815–50.

Limerick Harbour Commissioners: minute books, pilot books, tonnage dues, 1823–.

Limerick House of Industry register, 1774–94.

St John's Hospital: minutes, correspondence, register of patients, accounts, 1816–1905.

Sir Vere Hunt papers, 1716–1818; Monteagle papers, 1605–1930; Coote papers, 1776–1843; miscellaneous deeds from solicitors' collections, 1624–1900.

Microfilm and database collections relevant to genealogical research in the Limerick area.

130   Linen Hall Library

Address	17 Donegall Square North Belfast BT1 5GD
Telephone	(01232) 321707
E-mail	info@linenhall.com
Enquiries to	The Librarian
Opening hours and facilities	9.30–5.30, Mon–Fri; 9.30–4.00, Sat; photocopying

Major collections

Archives of the library, 1791–, including manuscript minutes of the Governors of the Library; wages books; minutes of various committees.

Manuscript meteorological records for Belfast, 1796–1906.

Joy MSS: selected materials for the annals of the province of Ulster, collected by Henry Joy, 18th century and early 19th century.

Minutes of the Belfast Literary Society, 1801–.

Minutes of Belfast Burns Society, 1931–.
Blackwood MSS: family history and pedigree collection compiled by R.W.H. Blackwood.
Belfast News Letter: index to births, marriages and deaths, 1738–1863.

131   Little Sisters of the Assumption

Address	Provincial House 42 Rathfarnham Road Dublin 6W
Telephone	(01) 490 9850
Fax	(01) 492 5740
E-mail	lsa@indigo.ie
Enquiries to	The Secretary
Opening hours and facilities	9.00–5.00, Mon–Fri; appointment advisable; photocopying

Major collections
Material relating to the history of the Little Sisters of the Assumption in Ireland, containing information on founders, initial formation houses, and individual houses in Ireland, Wales and Ethiopia. Correspondence from the province to the motherhouse in Paris; general Chapter meetings; meetings in the province; and general correspondence.

132   Loreto Sisters (Irish Branch of the Institute of the Blessed Virgin Mary)

Address	Loreto Abbey Rathfarnham Dublin 14
Telephone	(01) 495 0156
Fax	(01) 495 0156
Enquiries to	The Archivist
Opening hours and facilities	By appointment; photocopying

Major collections
Archives of the Irish branch of IBVM, 1822–.
Material relating to Mary Ward (1585–1645), foundress of IBVM and papers of Francis Teresa Ball (1794–1861), foundress of the Irish branch of IBVM, usually called Loreto.
Material relating to the administration of the Institute at Generalate and Provincial level.
Biographical material relating to individual members of the Institute. Collection of published work.

133   Louth County Library

Address	Roden Place Dundalk
Telephone	(042) 933 5457
Enquiries to	The Librarian
Opening hours and facilities	10.00–1.00, 2.00–5.00, Tue–Sat; photocopying; microfilm reader/printer

Major collections
Poor Law Guardians minute books: Dundalk, 1839–1924; Drogheda, 1839–1919; Ardee, 1851–1924.
County Louth Grand Jury records, 1830–98.
Ardee: Corporation minutes, 1661–1841; Borough Court books, 1746–75; Clerk of the Court's minute book, 1889–1963; poll book, 1768.
Miscellaneous County Louth estate rentals and accounts, 1857–86. Records of Dundalk Free Library, 1869–1911; Mechanics Institute Library, 1832–57; Dundalk Gas Light Company, 1856–98; Dundalk Premier Utility Society, 1929–38; Great Northern Railway, 1915–46; Board of Superintendents of County Louth Jail, 1832–62; North Louth Local Defence Force, 1940–1.
Large reference collection of local newspapers, journals and maps.

134   Archbishop Marsh's Library

Address	St Patrick's Close Dublin 8
Telephone	(01) 454 3511
Fax	(01) 454 3511

E-mail	marshlib@iol.ie
Website address	www.kst.dit.ie/marsh
Enquiries to	The Keeper
Opening hours and facilities	10.00–12.45, 2.00–5.00, Mon, Wed–Fri; 10.30–12.30, Sat
Guides	N.J.D. White, *Catalogue of the Manuscripts remaining in Marsh's Library, Dublin* (Dublin, 1913)

Major collections

*c.*300 manuscripts from the collections of Narcissus Marsh (1638–1713), Archbishop of Armagh; Elie Bouhéreau (1643–1719), the first Keeper of the Library; and Dudley Loftus (1619–95), jurist and orientalist. The manuscripts, collected by Loftus and purchased by Archbishop Marsh, relate mainly to Irish history.

The manuscripts include a volume of the Lives of the Irish Saints, in Latin, dating from *c.*1400; a Sarum Processional from the Church of St John the Evangelist, Dublin, 15th century; and two volumes of Bishop Bedell's original translation of the Old Testament into Irish.

Collection of letters in French to Dr Bouhéreau, a Huguenot refugee, before he came to Ireland, 17th century.

Music manuscripts including 17th century part books and a book of lute tabulature, late 16th century.

135 Mary Immaculate College

Address	South Circular Road Limerick
Telephone	(061) 314923
Fax	(061) 313632
E-mail	mary.brassil@mac.ul.ie
Enquiries to	The Librarian
Opening hours and facilities	9.00–10.00, during term time; 9.00–5.00, during vacations; photocopying

Major collections

Irish Folklore Commission collection.

136 Masonic Order (Grand Lodge of Ancient, Free & Accepted Masons of Ireland)

Address　　　　Freemasons' Hall
　　　　　　　　Molesworth Street
　　　　　　　　Dublin 2

Telephone　　　(01) 676 1337/662 4485

Fax　　　　　　(01) 662 5101

E-mail　　　　glfi@iol.ie

Enquiries to　　The Librarian and Archivist

Opening hours　Mon–Fri; by appointment;
and facilities　photocopying; photography; microfilming

Major collections

Grand Lodge records: membership registers of 2,300 lodges and minute books of various administrative bodies. Correspondence files relating to Irish Masonic lodges at home and overseas, early 18th–20th century.

Subordinate Lodge records: minute books and other effects of individual lodges (*c.*300 individual collections).

Records of Masonic benevolent institutions including the records of the Masonic Female Orphan School (founded 1792) and the Masonic Boys' School (founded 1867). Charity Petitions, 18th–20th century. Restricted access.

Microfilms and photocopies of Irish Masonic records held in other custodies, 18th–20th century.

137 Mayo County Council

Address　　　　Áras an Chontae
　　　　　　　　The Mall
　　　　　　　　Castlebar
　　　　　　　　County Mayo

Telephone　　　(094) 24444

Fax　　　　　　(094) 23937

Enquiries to　　The Archivist

Opening hours   9.00–1.00, 2.00–5.00; Mon–Fri; by appointment;
and facilities   photocopying

Major collections
Board of Guardians minutes: Swinford, 1883, 1893.
Poor Law archives: Ballinrobe, 1850–1919.
Rural District Council minutes: Castlebar, 1909–17, and Ballinrobe, 1903–25.
Urban District Council archives: Castlebar, 1901–, and Ballina, 1901–.
Mayo County Council archives including Council minutes, 1899–, and series from the various administrative sections of the Council, such as finance, housing, motor tax, roads and sanitary services, *c.* 1933–.

138   Meath County Library

Address   Railway Street
Navan
County Meath

Telephone   (046) 21134/21451

Enquiries to   The County Librarian

Opening hours   9.30–1.00, 2.00–5.00, Mon–Fri; 10.00–12.30, Sat;
and facilities   7.00–8.30, Tue & Thur; photocopying

Major collections
Board of Guardians minute books: Dunshaughlin Union, 1839–1921; Kells Union, 1839–1922; Navan Union, 1839–1921; Oldcastle Union, 1870–1920; Trim Union, 1839–1921.
Rural District Council minute books: Kells, 1899–1923; Navan, 1899–1925; Dunshaughlin, 1899–1925; Ardee, 1899–1925.
Meath County Council: minutes, accounts, correspondence, valuation books, 1904–60.
Navan Urban District Council: minutes, accounts, correspondence, 1920–50.
Meath County Library Committee records, 1931–.
Board of Health: minute books 1934–42; Public Assistance record books, 1920–44.
Meath County Infirmary, Navan: records, 1809–1960.
Navan Town Commissioners: minutes, 1880–1902.
Kells Urban District Council: minutes, accounts, valuation books, committee minutes, 1897–1970.

Kells Town Commissioners: minutes, accounts, wages and expenditure records, 1842–1906.
Claytons Woollen Mills, Navan: records, 1919–66.

139   Meath Diocesan Archives

Address	The Cathedral Mullingar County Westmeath
Telephone	(044) 48338
Fax	(044) 40780
E-mail	MULLCATH@iol.ie
Enquiries to	The Archivist
Opening hours and facilities	10.00–5.00, Mon–Fri, by appointment; photocopying

Major collections
Documents, exemplaria, correspondence, leases and other material relating to diocesan affairs.
Incomplete series of baptism and marriage records on microfilm and computer, 18th century–.

140   Medical Missionaries of Mary

Address	Beechgrove Drogheda County Louth
Telephone	(041) 983 7512
Enquiries to	The Archivist
Opening hours and facilities	Postal enquiry only; photocopying

Major collections
Correspondence and other documents relating to the foundation of the congregation and its administration and works, 1937–.

141 Met Éireann (Irish Meteorological Service)

Address   Glasnevin Hill
                   Dublin 9

Telephone   (01) 806 4200

Fax   (01) 806 4247

E-mail   met.eireann@met.ie

Enquiries to   The Head of Administration

Opening hours   By appointment
and facilities

Major collections
Manuscript climatological registers from various Irish stations, mid–19th
   century–.
Administrative files of the Metereological Service, 1936–.
Papers of Dr Leo Wenzel Pollak, former member of the Meteorological
   Service (b. Prague 1888, d. Dublin 1964).

142 Michael Davitt National Memorial Museum

Address   Land League Place
                   Straide
                   County Mayo

Telephone   (094) 31022

Enquiries to   The Curator

Opening hours   10.00–6.00, April–October
and facilities

Guides   Introductory leaflets

Major collections
Miscellaneous papers relating to Michael Davitt (1846–1906): addresses
   of welcome, 1882–95; letters and cards, 1898–1905; police reports,
   1879–82; photographs, 1879–82; diary of the Governor of Dartmoor
   Prison, 1870–82.

143   Military Archives

Address	Cathal Brugha Barracks Rathmines Dublin 6
Telephone	(01) 497 5499/804 6457
Fax	(01) 497 4027
Enquiries to	The Military Archivist
Opening hours and facilities	10.00–4.00, by appointment; photocopying

Major collections

Collins papers relating to the formation of the I.R.A., 1919–22.

Liaison papers concerning the period between the Truce and the Civil War, containing correspondence between the Irish and British authorities relating to breaches of the Truce.

Civil War material including operational and intelligence reports from all commands, July 1922–Mar 1924; copies of radio reports between all commands and the Commander in Chief, Adjutant General, Quartermaster General and Director of Intelligence; Railway Protection Corps, Internment Camps, Press and Publicity and Special Infantry Corps files; orders, instructions and memoranda; documents captured from anti-Treaty forces dealing with operational and intelligence matters; Department of Defence files, 1922–5; complete army census, Nov 1922.

Army Crisis, 1924; Army Organisation Board, 1926; Military Mission to U.S.A., 1926–7; Temporary Plans Division, 1928; Volunteer Force files, 1934–9; internees files; minutes of G.H.Q. Staff Conferences, 1925–39; Department of Defence files, 1925–47.

Director of Intelligence, Director of Operations, Construction Corps, and Air Defence Command files, 1939–45; G.H.Q. Unit Journals; look out posts log books; minutes of G.H.Q. Conferences and Controller of Censorship files; Air Raid Precautions files.

Director of Operations, 1945–74; Air Corps and Naval Service; United Nations Service, 1958–90; Department of Defence Files, 1947–61.

Copies of handbooks and military publications including *An t-Oglach* and *An Cosantoir.*

c. 700 private paper collections of retired army personnel.

144   Millmount Museum

Address	Millmount Drogheda County Louth
Telephone	(041) 983 3097
Fax	(041) 984 1599
Enquiries to	The Supervisor
Opening hours and facilities	10.00–6.00, Mon–Sat; 2.30–6.00, Sun; also by appointment

Major collections

Millmount Museum: catalogue of contents.

Drogheda Union (Board of Guardians): minutes, accounts, register of children, 1858–1923.

River Boyne Company: journal 1790–5.

Drogheda Rowing Club: minute book, 1895–1914.

Drogheda Carpenters and Joiners' Society: minute book, 1867–.

Drogheda Brick and Stone Layers' Society: account book, 1895–1948.

145   Missionary Sisters of the Holy Rosary

Address	Generalate House 23 Cross Avenue Booterstown County Dublin
Telephone	(01) 288 1708
Fax	(01) 283 6308
E-mail	mshrgen@indigo.ie
Enquiries to	The Archivist
Opening hours and facilities	10.00–5.00, Mon–Fri, by appointment; photocopying

Major collections

Correspondence and documents relating to the foundation of the congregation, 1920–4.

Official documents, reports and correspondence with the Congregation for Religious (Rome), with ecclesiastical authorities and with Mission Houses.

Private correspondence of members of the congregation, including letters of the founder, Bishop Shanahan.

Community annals covering the opening of all missions and their development. General records of the administration and growth of the congregation. Circular letters, bulletins, newsletters and magazines. Biographical material/necrologies.

146 Monaghan County Library

Address	County Library Headquarters The Diamond Clones County Monaghan
Telephone	(047) 51143
Fax	(047) 51863
E-mail	monaghan@tinet.ie
Enquiries to	The County Librarian
Opening hours and facilities	By appointment; photocopying

Major collections

Monaghan Grand Jury Presentments, 1811–59.

Material relating to Monaghan County Infirmary and to Monaghan and Clones Fever Hospitals, 1850–1939.

Records of Carrickmacross, Castleblayney and Clones Poor Law Unions, including minutes and correspondence, 1840–1933; material relating to home assistance and indoor relief, 1909–43.

Monaghan Urban and Rural District Councils minute books, 1899–1968. County Monaghan revised valuation lists, 1902–41.

Crossmaglen Rural District Council minute books and general ledger, 1899–1907.

147   Monaghan County Museum

Address   The Hill
Monaghan

Telephone   (047) 82928

Fax   (047) 71189

Enquiries to   The Curator

Opening hours   11.00–1.00, 2.00–5.00, Tues–Fri; Mon by
and facilities   appointment; photocopying

Major collections

Papers from various estates, mostly in County Monaghan but also in County Louth and County Dublin, 18th–20th century.

Marron collection of extracts from records relating to County Monaghan in the Public Record Office, London; State Paper Office, Dublin; Marquis of Bath's archives in Longleat House, Wiltshire.

Monaghan County Council: minutes, rate books, ledgers, 1899–1959.

Miscellaneous records of Monaghan Urban District Council, Clones Petty Sessions, Monaghan County Infirmary, Castleblayney Workhouse, 19th–20th century.

Legal papers relating to the Local Authority (Labourers) Act.

Small collections of papers of Charles Gavan Duffy (1816–1903) and Senator Thomas Toal, 1911–42, and other miscellaneous items.

148   Monaghan Urban District Council

Address   Town Hall
1 Dublin Street
Monaghan

Telephone   (047) 82600

Fax   (047) 84549

Enquiries to   The Town Clerk

Opening hours   By appointment
and facilities

Major collections

Records of Monaghan Corporation, 18th–19th century.

Records of Monaghan Urban District Council, 19th–20th century.

149   Moravian Church in Ireland

Address	25 Church Road Gracehill Ballymena County Antrim
Telephone	(0266) 653141
Enquiries to	The Minister
Opening hours and facilities	By appointment

Major collections

Records (registers of members, baptisms, marriages and burials; minutes; accounts; diaries; deeds) of the Moravian churches in Ballinderry, County Antrim, 1754–1889; Kilwarlin, County Down, 1834–1903; Gracehill, County Antrim, 1719–1987; Dublin, 1748–1980; Cootehill, County Cavan, 1894–1915.

Microfilm copies of these records are available in the Public Record Office of Northern Ireland.

150   Mount Melleray Abbey

Address	Cappoquin County Waterford
Telephone	(058) 54404
Fax	(058) 52140
Enquiries to	The Archivist
Opening hours and facilities	Postal enquiry only
Guides	Pádraig Ó Machain, *Catalogue of Irish manuscripts in Mount Melleray Abbey, County Waterford* (Dublin, DIAS, School of Celtic Studies, 1991).

Major collections

Cistercian antiphoner, 12th century. Cistercian graduale. Latin Vulgate version of the Bible, 13th or 14th century. Collection of Irish manuscripts. Canon W. Burke Collection of historical papers.

151 Muckross House

Address	Killarney County Kerry
Telephone	(064) 31440
Fax	(064) 33926
E-mail	mucros@iol.ie
Website address	www.muckross-house.ie
Enquiries to	The Research and Education Officer
Opening hours and facilities	9.00–5.30, Mon–Fri; closed for a week at Christmas; research application forms available for appointments; photocopying

Major collections
Portion of the Kenmare papers relating to the Browne family, formerly Earls of Kenmare

152 National Archives

Address	Bishop Street Dublin 8
Telephone	(01) 407 2300
Fax	(01) 407 2333
E-mail	mail@national archives.ie
Website address	nationalarchives.ie
Enquiries to	The Director
Opening hours and facilities	10.00–5.00, Mon–Fri; photocopying; photography; microfilming
Guides	*Short Guide to the National Archives* (forthcoming); *Short Guide to the Public Record Office of Ireland* (1964); *Reports of the Director of the National Archives* (forthcoming); *Reports of the National Archives Advisory Council, nos.1– (1990–). Reports of the Deputy Keeper of the Public Records in Ireland, nos. 1–59* (1869–1962) and 60 (forthcoming), nos. 55–60 relate

mainly to records accessioned since 1922, nos. 1–54 refer largely to records destroyed in 1922. The records which were destroyed are more fully described in A *Guide to the Records Deposited in the Public Record Office of Ireland,* ed. Herbert Wood (Dublin, 1919). In the case of the National Archives the information contained in *Manuscript Sources for the History of Irish Civilisation* (Boston, 1965 and 1979) is confined largely to archives accessioned from private sources. Archives deposited in the National Archives through the Business Records Survey of the Irish Manuscripts Commission are reported on in *Irish Economic and Social History,* vols 10– (1985–). Information leaflets, educational facsimiles and off-prints of articles are available for the following topics: Some facts about the National Archives, Sources for genealogy, Sources for local history, Sources for maritime history, Sources for the history of education, Sources for medieval history, Records of the Irish Record Commission, Fenian Documents, Trade Union and labour–related records, Workers in Union, the National School System.

Major collections

Almost all the archives accessioned by the Public Record Office of Ireland before 1922 were destroyed by fire and explosion during the Civil War in June 1922.

Records of Government Departments: The Taoiseach (formerly President of the Executive Council) including records of Dáil Éireann, 1919–22, and Government minutes and associated files, 1922–; Agriculture and Food (originally Agriculture and Technical Instruction), 1899–; Education, including records of the Commissioners of National Education, 1831–1924, the Commissioners of Intermediate Education, 1897–1918, and the modern Department, 1922–; Energy (formerly part of Industry and Commerce), 1920s–; Environment, including orders of the Poor Law Commissioners and the Local Government Board, 1838–1922, and records of the former Department of Local Government and Public Health, 1922–; Finance, 1922–; Foreign Affairs (formerly External Affairs), including records of embassies and consulates in other countries 1919 –; Gaeltacht (originally part of the former Department of Lands), 1929–; Health (originally part of the former Department of Local Government and Public Health), 1920s–; Industry and Commerce, 1922–; Justice (originally Home Affairs), 1922–; Labour (formerly part of Industry and Commerce), 1920s–; The Marine, including records of the former Department of Fisheries and its precursors, 1845–; Social Welfare (formerly parts of Industry and Commerce and the former Department of Local Government and Public Health), 1919–; Tourism, Transport and Communications (formerly parts of Industry and Commerce, the pre–1922 Post Office, and the former Department of Posts and Telegraphs), 1900–. *(Note:* the records of the Department of Defence are held in the Military Archives, q.v.)

Records of other government offices and state agencies including: Chief Secretary's Office, 1790–1924, and its constituent departments, including the Convict Department 1778–1922, the Privy Council Office, 1800–1922, and the Chief Crown Solicitor's Office, mostly 1859–90; Office of the Attorney General, 1922–; Board of Health (Cholera papers), 1832–4; Census of population returns, 1901 and 1911 (complete for all 32 counties) and 1821–51 (fragments for a few counties); Charitable Donations and Bequests, 19th–20th century; Companies Registration Office, 1921–; Office of the Comptroller and Auditor General, 1920s–; Customs and Excise, 1778–1837; Fair Trade Commission, 1953–; Famine Relief Commission, 1845–7; Office of the Governor General, 1922–8; Labour Court, 1946–; National Archives (formerly the Public Record Office of Ireland and the State Paper Office), mostly 1867–; Ordnance Survey, 1824–; Patents Office, 1927–; Office of the Secretary to the President, 1937–; Prison administration records, including the Government Prisons Office, 1836–80, and the General Prisons Board, 1877–1928; Prison registers, 19th–20th century; Proclamations, 17th–19th century; Office of Public Works, 1831–, and its precursors, the Directors General of Inland Navigation, mostly 1800–31, and the Civil Buildings Commissioners, 1802–31; Quit Rent Office, 17th–20th century; Registry of Friendly Societies, c.1890–; Royal Hospital Kilmainham, 1684–1829; Shipping agreements and crew lists, 1863–; Tithe Applotment Books, 1828–37; Valuation Office and Boundary Survey, 1827–.

Court and probate records including: Supreme Court, 1924–; Court of Criminal Appeal, 1924; High Court, 1900–13 and 1922–; Probate Office of the High Court (formerly the Principal Probate Registry) and District Probate Registries, mostly 20th century; Circuit Court, Central Criminal Court, County Courts, Grand Juries etc. (transferred by County Registrars, formerly Clerks of the Crown and Peace), mostly late 19th–20th century; Petty Sessions Courts, mostly 1851–1922; Incumbered Estates Court, Landed Estates Court, Chancery Land Judges, rentals etc., mostly 1850–82; Dáil Éireann Courts, 1920–2; Chancery pleadings, 16th–17th century; a few plea rolls, 14th–15th century.

Registers of baptisms, marriages and burials of the Church of Ireland including: original registers of a few parishes; microfilms of surviving registers of parishes located mainly in dioceses of the south and west of the 26 counties.

Transcripts, calendars, abstracts and indexes of archives which were destroyed in 1922, including: Irish Record Commission (1810–30) calendars of court records, 13th–19th century; Ferguson extracts from Exchequer records, 13th–18th century; Lodge abstracts from Chancery patent rolls, mainly 17th century; Betham, Crosslé, Groves, Grove-White and Thrift collections of genealogical abstracts, mostly 17th–19th century.

In addition to the above, the National Archives holds records accessioned from many other sources, including harbour boards, health boards, hospitals, schools, charities, trade unions, business firms, solicitors' offices, estate offices and private individuals.

153   National Botanic Gardens

Address	Glasnevin Dublin 9
Telephone	(01) 837 4388/ 837 7596/ 837 1636/ 837 1637
Fax	(01) 836 0080
E-mail	nbg@indigo.ie
Enquiries to	The Librarian
Opening hours and facilities	By appointment; photocopying
Guides	*Occasional Papers. National Botanic Gardens, Glasnevin, Dublin,* Nos. 1, 3 and 4 contain information on archival collections.

Major collections

Official correspondence of the Director, *c.*1870–.

Moore papers: photostat copies of family papers and official documents relating to Dr David Moore and Sir Frederick Moore, *c.*1838–1922.

Augustine Henry papers, 1880–1930: annotated books; manuscripts; notebooks (including tree books of Henry J. Elwes); Chinese diaries, 1880–99; annotated proofsheets of Elwes' & Henry's *Trees of Great Britain and Ireland, 1906–13.*

Botanical correspondence of Natural History Section of National Museum (transferred to National Botanic Gardens in 1970): principal correspondents are N. Colgan, R.L. Praeger, R.A. Phillips and J. Muir.

Watercolours: extensive collection of over 1,500 watercolours of plants cultivated in the Botanic Gardens, 1880–1920, by Lydia Shackleton, Josephine Humphries and Alice Jacob; watercolours by George Victor du Noyer; watercolours of European plants by the Hon Frederica Plunkett and the Hon. Katherine Plunkett, *c.*1880 (see *Occasional Papers* 3); pen and ink sketches of Irish plants by S. Rosamond Praeger (original drawings for books by her brother, Robert L. Praeger), Burmese plants (mainly orchids), 1900–22, by Lady Charlotte Wheeler–Cuffe.

National College of Art and Design *see* National Irish Visual Arts Library

154   National Gallery of Ireland

Address	Merrion Square Dublin 2
Telephone	(01) 661 5133
Fax	(01) 661 5372
Enquiries to	The Librarian & Curator of the Yeats Collection
Opening hours and facilities	Postal enquiry only

Major collections

National Gallery archives: Gallery papers from the foundation in the 1860s. Manuscript material on some artists; manuscript material relating to the provenance of paintings in the collection.

Jack B. Yeats archive including miscellaneae, sketchbooks, and the artist's library, together with books belonging to his father, wife and sisters: *c.* 200 sketchbooks documenting places visited in England, Ireland, New York and Europe, and the characters observed, 1897–1953; all the artist's published writings, his manuscripts, workbooks, catalogues, presscuttings, postcards, and scrapbooks.

155   National Irish Visual Arts Library

Address	100 Thomas Street Dublin 8
Telephone	(01) 636 4360
Fax	(01) 636 4207
E-mail	annehodge@ncad.ie
Website address	www.ncad.ie
Enquiries to	The Administrator
Opening hours and facilities	10.00–1.00, 2.00–5.00, Tues, Wed, Fri; 2.00–8.00, Thurs; photocopying; photography

Major collections

Over 2000 files of information on 20th century Irish artists: presscuttings, catalogues, ephemera and some manuscript material.

Similar files on galleries and related areas: public art, art collections, art and disability, design, craft, fashion.

Library of Evie Hone (1894–1955) including some manuscript material and sketches.

Egan collection: scrapbooks relating to the running of a Dublin gallery in the 1920s.

Records of the Cultural Relations Committee, 1949–52.

Archives of the National College of Art and Design: records of all enrolled students, 1877–1940s; reports and other material relating to the administration of the College, 20th century.

156   National Library of Ireland

Address	2/3 Kildare Street Dublin 2
Telephone	(01) 603 0200
Fax	(01) 676 6690
Enquiries to	The Director
Opening hours and facilities	10.00–8.30, Mon–Wed; 10.00–4.30, Thurs–Fri; 10.00–12.30, Sat.; Manuscripts are not issued 12.30–

2.00 and 5.00–6.00. Readers' tickets, for which identification is required, are issued in the main Library
building; photography

Guides   R.J. Hayes (ed.), *Manuscript Sources for the History of
Irish Civilisation* (Boston, 1965), and *Supplement*
(Boston, 1978); *Catalogue of Irish manuscripts in the
National Library of Ireland* (Dublin, 1967–); Noel
Kissane (ed.), *Treasures of the National Library of
Ireland* (Drogheda, 1994); major accessions noted in
annual *Report of the Council of Trustees of the National
Library of Ireland.*

Major collections
The collection amounts to 65,000 catalogued manuscripts comprising
750,000 individual items. There is also a special collection of 28,000
deeds. In addition there are a number of collections of estate papers
which have not yet been fully processed. The collection is composed
almost entirely of material of Irish interest. It is extremely diverse and
the following outline is no substitute for a careful study of the cata-
logues.
Estate papers constitute the main component of the collection. Among the
more notable estates represented are Balfour (Counties Louth and
Meath), Bellew (County Galway), Castletown (County Laois), Clements
(Counties Leitrim and Donegal), Clonbrock (County Galway),
Conyngham (Counties Meath, Donegal, Clare and Limerick), Coolatin
(County Wicklow), de Freyne (County Roscommon), de Vesci (County
Laois), Doneraile (County Cork), Farnham (County Cavan), Fingal
(County Dublin), ffrench (County Galway), Gormanston (County
Meath), Headford (County Meath), Inichquin (County Clare), Lismore
(County Waterford), Louth (Counties Meath, Louth, Monaghan and
Kildare), Mahon (County Galway), Mansfield (County Kildare),
Monteagle (County Limerick), O'Hara (County Sligo), Ormond
(Counties Kilkenny and Tipperary), Powerscourt (County Wicklow),
Prior-Wandesforde (County Kilkenny), Sarsfield (County Cork),
Wicklow (County Wicklow), Wynne (County Wicklow). Most of the col-
lections date from the 17th to the 20th century but the Ormond papers
include a collection of deeds extending back to the arrival of the
Normans in the 12th century.
The collection represents most of the nationalist movements from the 18th
century onwards, and includes papers of Wolfe Tone, Daniel O'Connell
and James Fintan Lalor. The Land War and Home Rule periods are represented by the papers of T.C. Harrington, T.P. Gill, William O'Brien,
J.F.X. O'Brien and John Redmond. The period 1916–23 is particularly

111

well documented and the collection includes papers of Sir Roger Casement, Erskine Childers, Thomas McDonagh, Bulmer Hobson, Eoin MacNeill, Dean T. O'Kelly and Patrick Pearse. The labour and trade union movements are represented by the papers of Thomas Johnson and William O'Brien.

The collection includes a number of substantial business archives including those of the Prior-Wandesforde Collieries, Castlecomer, Avoca Mines and Locke's Distillery, Kilbeggan.

The Kilmainham Papers consist of 377 volumes of records of the commanders-in-chief of the forces in Ireland, and provide detailed information on recruitment, personnel, supplies, encampments and movements of troops for the period 1780–1890.

Among the writers who are represented are Richard Brinsley Sheridan, Maria Edgeworth, Canon Sheehan, George Moore, John Millington Synge, George Bernard Shaw, Sean O'Casey, Patrick Kavanagh, Brendan Behan, Benedict Kiely, James Plunkett, Hugh Leonard and Tom McIntyre. Of particular importance are the large collection of papers of W.B. Yeats and the James Joyce/Paul Leon papers.

The collection of Gaelic manuscripts amounts to 1236 volumes or folders, dating from the 14th century onwards. The most notable accession was a collection of 178 volumes purchased at the Phillipps sale in 1931. Subject area represented are genealogy, hagiography, religion, medicine, law and *dinnseanchas* (place-lore). The bardic tradition is represented by the earliest surviving example of a book of praise poetry, the 14th century *duanaire* of Tomas Mag Shamhradhain of Tullyhaw, Co. Cavan, known as the Book of Magauran. Among the later writers whose work is represented are Aodhagán Ó Rathaille, Peader Ó Doirnin, Eoghan Ruadh Ó Súilleabháin, Brian Merriman and Tomas Ó Criomhtháin.

There is an extensive collection of maps and plans of Irish interest over half of which are estate maps which were acquired with estate collections. They are supplemented by 4,000 file copies of estate maps produced by the Dublin firm of surveyors, Brownrigg, Longfield and Murray in the period 1775–1833, which include material for most counties. Notable items in the map collection include a map of Europe in a 12th century copy of the Topographia Hiberniae of Giraldus Cambrensis, maps by Francis Jobson and Richard Bartlett documenting the Tudor conquest, and plans of fortifications in the period 1685–92 by Captain Thomas Phillips and the Huguenot engineer John Goubet. Also of interest are a set of 18th century copies of William Petty's Down Survey, a set of over 200 coloured maps of mail coach roads, 1805–16, and a set of maps of the bogs of Ireland, 1810–13.

The National Library also has an extensive collection of microfilm copies of material of Irish interest in archives and libraries overseas, much of it relating to the early medieval period.

157 National Maritime Museum of Ireland

Address   Haigh Terrace
               Dun Laoghaire
               County Dublin

Telephone   (01) 280 0969

Enquiries to   The Honorary Archivist

Opening hours By appointment; photocopying; photography
and facilities

Major collections
Records of the Maritime Institute of Ireland (parent body of the National Maritime Museum): minutes of the Council, 1941–, and the Executive Committee, 1941–82; papers of the Honorary Research Officer, 1947–91; records of public meetings and other activities, 1941 Minutes of the Museum Management Committee, 1978–.
Chart collection, photographic collection and press cuttings collection.

158 National Museum of Ireland

Address   Kildare Street
               Dublin 2

Telephone   (01) 677 7444

Fax   (01) 676 6116

Enquiries to   The Registrar

Opening hours 10.00–5.00, Tue–Fri; by appointment;
and facilities photocopying; photography

Major collections
Correspondence relating to the administration of the Museum and the acquisition of items now in the collections.
Archives of the Natural History Museum including notebooks and journals of naturalists whose collections are held by the Museum, 1850–.

159 National Photographic Archive

Address	Meeting House Square Temple Bar Dublin 2
Telephone	(01) 603 0200
Fax	(01) 677 7451
E-mail	photoarchive@nli.ie
Website	www.heanet.ie/natlib/
Enquiries to	The Curator
Opening hours and facilities	10.00–5.00, Mon–Fri; access to the Reading Room by appointment; reader's ticket required; reprographic services include the provision of photographic prints, transparencies and slides
Guides	Sarah Rouse, *Into the light. An illustrated guide to the photographic collections of the National Library of Ireland* (Dublin, 1998); general information leaflets

Major collections

Collections of portrait and postcard studios include the Lawrence collection (40,000 glass negatives of topographical scenes, 1870–1914), Stereo Pairs collection (3,059 glass negatives, mainly picturesque views, 1860–83), Eblana collection (3,000 glass negatives of topographical scenes, 1870–90), Eason collection (4,000 glass negatives for Eason postcard series, 1900–40), Valentine collection (3,000 glass negatives for the Valentine postcard series, 1900–60), Poole collection (60,000 glass negatives from the studio of A.H. Poole, Waterford, 1884–1954), Keogh collection (330 glass negatives of Dublin, 1915–30, from the Keogh Brothers studio), Morgan collection (aeriel views of Ireland, mid–1950s), Cardall collection (5,000 negatives for Cardall postcard series, 1950s–60s), Wiltshire collection (1,330 images taken by Elinor Wiltshire, mainly of Dublin, 1951–70s).

Other important photographic collections include the Clonbrock collection (3,500 glass plates taken by the Dillon Family, Barons Clonbrock, 1860–1930), O'Dea collection (railways in Ireland, 1937–66), Wynne collection (County Mayo, 1867–1960).

Smaller collections include good coverage of events during 1916, the War of Independence and the Civil War, as well as other political and social events.

Over 250 photographic albums covering a wide range of subjects.

160   National Theatre Archive

Address   The Abbey Theatre
26 Lower Abbey Street,
Dublin 1

Telephone   (01) 887 2200

Fax   (01) 872 9177

Enquiries to   The Archivist

Opening hours   By appointment only
and facilities

Major collections
Archives of the National Theatre Society Limited and related material on
the history and development of theatre in Ireland, which provides a con-
text for the history and development of the Abbey Theatre, dating from
its foundation in 1904. The collection includes handbills, posters, scripts,
prompt scripts, programmes, presscuttings, music scores; early stage
management records; stage plans and drawings, production photographs,
model boxes; a large collection of administrative records including log-
books of plays received, financial records and correspondence.

161   National University of Ireland

Address   49 Merrion Square
Dublin 2

Telephone   (01) 676 7246/676 3429

Fax   (01) 661 9665

E-mail   registrar@nui.ie

Enquiries to   The Registrar

Opening hours   9.15–1.00, 2.15–5.00, Mon–Fri; by appointment;
and facilities

Major collections
Royal University of Ireland: minutes of the Senate, 1880–1908, of the
Standing Committee, 1883–1909, and of the Medical, Library and other
occasional committees, 1891–1908; financial records, 1881–1908; copy

letter books, 1880–1908; matriculation application forms and printed matter including calendars and examination papers, 1883–1909.

National University of Ireland: minutes of the Senate, Standing Committee, Finance Committee, and General Board of Studies with supporting documents, 1908–; correspondence, 1909–; statutes, 1911–; printed matter including calendars, examination results, sessional and honours lists, 1911–.

162 National University of Ireland, Cork Boole Library

Address	University College Cork
Telephone	(021) 903180
Fax	(021) 273428
E-mail	c.quinn@ucc.ie
Website address	booleweb.ucc.ie/search/subject/archives/archives.htm
Enquiries to	The Archivist
Opening hours and facilities	9.30–1.00, 2.30–4.45, Mon–Fri; early closing 4.15, June–Sept; appointment necessary; photocopying; photography
Guides	P. de Brún, *Clár lámhscríbhinní Gaeilge Choláiste Ollscoile Chorcaí: cnuasach Thorna* (1967). B. Ó Conchuir, 'Scríbhaithe Chorcaí, 1700–1850', *An Clochomhar* (1982). B. Ó Conchuir, *Clár lámhscríbhinní Gaeilge Choláiste Ollscoile Chorcaí: cnuasach Uí Mhurchú* (Dublin Institute for Advanced Studies, 1991). P. Bull, 'William O'Brien MSS in the library of UCC', *JCHAS* lxxv (1970).

Major collections

Papers, mainly academic, of former presidents and professors including Tadhg Ó Donnchadha, Alfred O'Rahilly, M.D. MacCarthy, Cormac Ó Cúilleanáin, Daniel Corkery and G. Boole.

Kinsale manorial records, 17th century; minutes of Cork Cuvierian Society; Grehan family papers; records relating to the Seward estate in Youghal, 19th–20th century; miscellaneous papers of William O'Brien; literary works of Patrick Galvin.

Attic Press collection, Bantry House collection, Peters photographic collection.

Collections of Gaelic manuscripts of Ó Murchadha, de Paor, Ó Cathalain and Ó Leighinn.

Torna MSS including material collected and transcribed by him.

163   National University of Ireland, Cork College Archives

Address	University Heritage Office University College Cork
Telephone	(021) 903552/902753
Fax	(021) 903555
E-mail	v.teehan@ucc.ie
Website	www.ucc.ie
Enquiries to	The College Archivist
Opening hours and facilities	10.00–5.00, Mon–Fri; by appointment; photocopying; photography

Major collections

Archives of University College, Cork, 1845–*c.*1960, reflecting the educational, administrative and social aspects of the College since its foundation as Queen's College Cork, including identifiable series originating from College offices such as the Office of the President, Vice–President, Registrar, Finance Officer and Secretary, College Engineer, and Librarian.

Admission records; recent examination results, 1930–.

Records relating to individual academic departments, *c.*1925–.

Computerised data base of title deeds of College buildings and lands, cross-referenced to the series of architectural maps and plans of the College.

Minute books of College committees, and of student clubs and societies.

College publications including staff newsletters, student magazines and pamphlets produced by the College. Reference collection of published work relevant to the College, its history, to individuals associated with the College, and the College's role in the community.

Collection of photographs documenting the evolution of the College, mid-19th century–.

Private paper collections of individuals associated with UCC including
Professor Aloys Fleischmann and Professor James Hogan.
UCC oral history collection.

National University of Ireland, Dublin *see* University College Dublin

164 National University of Ireland, Galway James Hardiman Library

Address	National University of Ireland Galway
Telephone	(091) 524411 ext. 3636
Fax	(091) 522394
E-mail	kieran@sulacco.library.ucg.ie
Website address	www.library.nuigalway.ie
Enquiries to	The Archivist
Opening hours and facilities	9.30–1.15, 2.30–5.00, Mon–Fri; appointment advisable; photocopying; photography by arrangement
Guides	Published work on the Corporation MSS can be found in Royal Commission on Historical Manuscripts, *10th Report* (1885), 380–520 and in various issues of the *Galway Archaeological & Historical Society Journal*. See M. Hayes–McCoy 'The Eyre Documents in University College Galway' in *GAHSJ* 20 (1942).

Major collections

Minute books of Galway Corporation, Galway Town Commissioners, 15th–19th century; minute books of Galway Urban Sanitary Authority, late 19th century.

The Hyde MSS Collection, bequeathed by Douglas Hyde, containing volumes of prose, poetry and various tracts penned by scribes, 18th century–, and including miscellaneous manuscripts of Douglas Hyde.

Manuscripts in the Irish language and items reflecting the Gaelic revival are included in collections such as the papers of Stiophán Bairéad and Tadgh Seoige.

Richie-Pickow collection of over 5,000 photographs and some traditional music material gathered by an American couple in Ireland, 1952–3.

Collections relating to academics and organizations within the College including papers of *An Stoc* newspaper, 1924–8; out letter book of Professor J.E. Cairnes, 1865–7; papers of Richard O'Doherty, professor of midwifery, 1849–76; papers of Mary O'Donovan, professor of history, 1914–57.

Landed estates collections including the Wilson Lynch family, Belvoir, County Clare, *c.*1860–1930; Eyre family, 1720–1857; O'Connor Donelan family, Sylane, Tuam, 1794–1930; O'Callighan collection (including papers relating to the Bodyke evictions); Castle Taylor, Ardrahan, County Galway; Daly family, Dunsandle, Loughrea; some material of the ffrench family of Ballyglunin.

Business collections including legal papers relating to the Clifden–Galway railway.

Political collections including those of James Fitzgerald-Kenney, Dr Byran Cusack and Frank J. Carty.

Theatre collections including those of the Druid Theatre and *An Taibhdearc*.

Private papers including papers relating to the will of Annie Barnacle; Stock letters, 1808–32; and many small collections.

165 National University of Ireland, Maynooth
Russell Library

Address	Maynooth County Kildare
Telephone	(01) 708 3890
Fax	(01) 628 6008
E-mail	Russell.Library@may.ie
Website address	www.may.ie/library
Enquiries to	The Librarian, Special Collections
Opening hours and facilities	9.30–1.00, Mon–Fri; appointment advisable; photography
Guides	Paul Walsh, *Catalogue of Irish manuscripts in Maynooth College Library* (Ma Nuad, 1943); Pádraig Ó Fiannachta, *Clár lamhscríbhinní Gaeilge Mha Nuad*, fasc. 2–8 (Ma Nuad, 1965–73); Pádraig Ó Fiannachta,

Leabharlanna na cleire II (Institiúid Ard–Leinn Bhaile Átha Cliath, 1980); Pádraig de Brún, *Lamhscríbhinní Gaeilge: treoirliosta* (Institiúid Ard-Leinn Bhaile Átha Cliath, 1988); R.W. Richardson (ed.) *The Salamanca letters: a catalogue of correspondence, 1691–1871* (Maynooth, 1995); Agnes Neligan *Maynooth Library Treasures* (Dublin, 1995).

Major collections

120 volumes of Irish manuscripts copied for or collected, *c.*1820, by Dr John Murphy, Bishop of Cork (1771–1847); includes romances, religious and secular poetry, sermons, translations of devotional works, lives of saints and genealogies.

*c.*100 Irish manuscripts collected by Eugene O'Curry (1796–1862), and additional material transcribed by him. 30 volumes of Irish manuscripts collected by Dr Laurence Renehan, President of the College (1845–57).

Illuminated manuscripts and books of hours; other manuscripts in Latin including liturgical works, commentaries on scripture and canon law, and student notebooks from Douay and Salamanca.

Manuscript material in English including Laurence Renehan's historical papers and transcripts, antiquarian papers of Fr J.F. Shearman, Canon O'Hanlon's notes for his *Lives of the Saints,* and literary items such as 'The Master', a play by Patrick Pearse.

National University of Ireland, Maynooth *see also* St Patrick's College, Maynooth

166   New Ross Port Company

Address	Harbour Office New Ross County Wexford
Telephone	(051) 421303
Fax	(051) 421294
Enquiries to	The Chief Executive
Opening hours and facilities	By appointment; photocopying

Major collections
Minute books, 1848–1986; shipping books, 1958–; letterbooks and corre-
    spondence, 1927–40, 1980–; register of vessels, 1848–91; register of
    mortgages, 1851–76; ledgers, 1848–1900 and other financial records.

167 Newbridge House

Address	Donabate
	County Dublin
Telephone	(01) 843 6534
Fax	(01) 846 2537
Enquiries to	The Curator
Opening hours and facilities	By appointment
Guides	Information leaflets available

Major collections
Newbridge House account books, 18th century; farm diary, 1840–2; land
    survey map, 1747.
Pilkington family papers including material relating to the life of John
    Pilkington; correspondence and memoirs of Laetitia Pilkington; and
    poems of Revd Matthew Pilkington corrected by Dean Swift, 18th cen-
    tury.
Cobbe family papers including the diary of Colonel Alexander Cobbe VC,
    1894, and the journal of Archbishop Charles Cobbe, 1742–3.

168 North Down Heritage Centre

Address	Town Hall
	Bangor Castle
	Bangor
	County Down
Telephone	(01247) 271200
Fax	(01247) 271370
Enquiries to	The Manager

| *Opening hours* | 10.20–4.30, Tue–Sat; 2.00–4.30, Sun; |
| *and facilities* | photocopying; photography |

Major collections

Miscellaneous local authority records relating especially to the harbour, gas supply and public health, early 20th century–.

Volume of 64 maps of the North Down and Strangford Lough areas by Thomas Raven, 17th century.

Memorabilia relating to Percy French.

169   Offaly County Library

Address	O'Connor Square
	Tullamore
Telephone	(0506) 46833/4
Fax	(0506) 52769
E-mail	colibrar@offalycoco.ie
Enquiries to	The County Librarian
Opening hours	By appointment; photocopying
and facilities	

Major collections

Board of Guardians minute books: Birr, 1910–15; Edenderry, 1879–1919; Parsonstown, 1839–1921; Tullamore, 1839–1921.

Rural District Council minute books: Birr, 1899–1928; Edenderry, 1913–28; Kilbeggan, 1889–1918; Roscrea, 1899–1917; Tullamore, 1899–1917.

King's County Council: accounts, personal ledgers, letters, hospital and County Infirmary records, 1837–1964.

170   Oireachtas Library

Address	Leinster House
	Kildare Street
	Dublin 2
Telephone	(01) 618 3412

Fax	(01) 618 4376
Enquiries to	The Librarian
Opening hours and facilities	Admission to the Library is normally restricted to members of the Oireachtas and Oireachtas officials. Members of the public will only be admitted by permission of the Ceann Comhairle [Speaker]. Access should then be arranged with the Librarian; photocopying

Major collections

Manuscript records of trials conducted by the Special Commission (Fenianism), 1866.

Miscellaneous reports on aspects of Irish affairs including ports, gaols, public records and the work of public offices, 17th–19th century.

171   Ordnance Survey of Northern Ireland

Address	Colby House Stranmillis Court Belfast BT9 5BJ
Telephone	(01232) 255755
Fax	(01232) 255700
E-mail	osni@nics.gov.uk
Website address	www.nics.gov.uk/doe/ordnance/ordnance.htm
Enquiries to	The Director
Opening hours and facilities	9.15–4.30, Mon–Fri;

Major collections

Major collection of maps and aerial films of Northern Ireland: 6" county series maps, 1830–1900; 6" and 25" county series maps, 1900–50; Irish grid series maps at all scales and aerial films, 1950–.

172   Ossory Diocesan Archives

Address	Sion House Kilkenny
Telephone	(056) 62448
Fax	(056) 63753
E-mail	diocoss@iol.ie
Enquiries to	The Bishop of Ossory
Opening hours and facilities	By appointment; photocopying

Major collections
Papers and correspondence of bishops and priests, 1639–.

173   Passionist Fathers

Address	St Paul's Retreat Mount Argus Kyeemagh Road Dublin 6W
Telephone	(01) 492 3165
Fax	(01) 492 1147
E-mail	passionistmtargus@tinet.ie
Enquiries to	The Archivist
Opening hours and facilities	By appointment; photocopying

Major collections
Archives of Mount Argus but including material relating to other Passionist houses in Ireland, Scotland and Botswana.
Records of Passionist personnel, 1805–; diary recording the early days of Mount Argus in 7 vols; chronicles; accounts; *Cross,* monthly magazine, 1910–80.
Journal by Revd Pius Devine of his journey through the Americas, 1880s, on a lecturing tour to reduce the debt of Mount Argus.

174 Patrician Brothers (Brothers of St Patrick)

Address   Patrician Generalate
Tullow Hill
Tullow
County Carlow

Telephone   (0503) 51190

Fax   (0503) 51900

Enquiries to   The Archivist

Opening hours and facilities   Postal enquiry; photocopying

Major collections

Material relating to the origins of the Patrician Brothers and to houses in Ireland, 1808–1960; in India, 1875–1960; in Australia, 1883–1960; in Papua New Guinea, 1960–; and in California, 1947–60.
Correspondence of the Superior General, 1880–1960.
Diaries and travel accounts of some members of the congregation.
Correspondence, mainly personal, notebooks and account books, 1829–1960.
Printed matter including chapter studies and constitutions, 1880–1986.

175 Pearse Museum

Address   St Enda's Park
Rathfarnham
Dublin 14

Telephone   (01) 493 4208

Fax   (01) 493 6120

Enquiries to   The Curator

Opening hours and facilities   10.00–1.00 daily; 2.00–5.30, Oct–Mar; 2.00–6.00, Apr–Sep

Major collections

Documents, photographs and personal effects relating to Patrick Pearse (1879–1916) and the history of St Enda's.

176   Presbyterian Historical Society

Address	Church House Fisherwick Place Belfast BT1 6DW
Telephone	(01232) 322284
Enquiries to	The Assistant Secretary
Opening hours and facilities	10.00–12.30, Mon–Fri; 2.00–4.00, Wed; photocopying
Guides	Annual *Bulletin of the Presbyterian Historical Society of Ireland*

Major collections

Records of the General Synod of Ulster and the Seceders and, since 1840, of the General Assembly of the Presbyterian Church in Ireland.

Records relating to some presbyteries and congregations; baptismal and marriage records of many congregations; files detailing records held by congregations.

Files on ministers of the Presbyterian Church in Ireland from 1613.

Writings by Presbyterian ministers.

Copies, by Tenison Groves, of census records.

Communion tokens and artefacts relating to Presbyterianism.

177   Presentation Sisters

Address	Presentation Mission House Lucan County Dublin
Telephone	(01) 628 0540/ 628 0305
Enquiries to	The Archivist
Opening hours and facilities	10.00–12.00, 2.00–5.30, Mon–Fri; by appointment; photocopying

Major collections

Material relating to Nano Nagle (18th century) and to the work of Presentation Sisters in Ireland, England, Africa, India and Pakistan, USA, Latin America and Slovakia. This includes annals, theses, correspondence and published work by Presentation Sisters.

178   Public Record Office of Northern Ireland

Address	66 Balmoral Avenue Belfast BT9 6NY
Telephone	(01232) 251318
Fax	(01232) 255999
E-mail	proni@doeni.gov.uk
Website address	proni.nics.gov.uk/index.htm
Enquiries to	The Head of Reader Services
Opening hours and facilities	9.15–4.45, Mon–Wed & Fri, 9.15–8.45, Thurs; annual closure for weeks in Nov/Dec; photocopying; microfilming
Guides	*Reports of the Deputy Keeper of the Records, 1923–87; Annual Report, 1991–5; Statutory Reports, 1995–.* Sectional lists on textile industry records, landed estate, tithes, church registers, maps and plans, electoral registers, and educational records. Recent publications include *Guide to Sources for Women's History, Guide to County Sources – Fermanagh, Armagh, Tyrone, Monaghan.* A full list of publications is available on request.

Major collections

Records of the principal departments of government from the 1920s: papers of the Northern Ireland Cabinet, 1922–.

Records of the Crown and County Courts, 18th century–; records of Borough, County, Urban and Rural District councils, 19th century–, and in some cases, 18th century–.

Ordnance Survey maps, 1830–1970; tithe applotment books, 1823–38; valuation records comprising maps and valuation lists, 1828–; records of the Boards of Guardians, 1838–1948; records of some 2,500 national schools, 1832–70.

Private records: landed estate records including title deeds, agents' reports, correspondence, rentals, household accounts, estate maps, valuations and surveys; large collection of business records including the records of over 250 linen companies; a wide range of solicitors' records, emigrant letters, and the papers of private societies and organisations, copies of church records, including parish registers.

179   Queen's University of Belfast

Address   Main Library
                     Queen's University
                     Belfast BT7 1NN

Telephone   (01232) 245133 (ext. 3607)

Fax   (01232) 247895

Enquiries to   The Special Collections Department

Opening hours   9.00–9.30, Mon–Fri during term; 9.00–5.00,
and facilities   Mon–Fri, 9.00–12.30, Sat during the summer vacation;
                     photocopying; photography

Guides   South and South East-Asian material noted in M.D.
                     Wainright, A *guide to Western manuscripts and docu-*
                     ments in the British Isles relating to South and South-
                     East Asia (London, 1965). Chinese material noted in N.
                     Matthews, *A guide to manuscripts and documents in the*
                     British Isles relating to the Far East (Oxford, 1977).
                     Australian material noted in P. Mander Jones, *Manu-*
                     scripts in the British Isles relating to Australia, New
                     Zealand and the Pacific (Canberra, 1972). African
                     material noted in N. Matthews, A *guide to manuscripts*
                     and documents in the British Isles relating to Africa
                     (Oxford, 1971). Mary T. Kelly (comp), *Papers of Helen*
                     Waddell: a calendar (1981).

Major collections

Archives of the University, 1909–, and of its predecessors, Queen's
    College, 1845–1909, Queen's University in Ireland, 1850–82, and the
    Royal University of Ireland, 1881–1909.
Scientific papers and correspondence of Thomas Andrews, 1828–76, and
    James Thomson, 1857–92.
Musical manuscripts collected and compiled by Edward Bunting,
    1792–1943. Original works by Sir Hamilton Harty, 1900–39.
Literary manuscripts of Arthur O'Shaughnessy, *c.*1863–70; Edith
    Somerville and Violet Martin, 1873–1948; Helen Waddell, 1909–50;
    Shan Bullock, 1889–1935.
Correspondence and classical and other papers of R.M. Henry, 1899–1941.
    Personal papers of Sir Robert Hart, Inspector General of the Chinese
    Imperial Maritime Customs, 1854–1908, and of Stanley F. Wright,
    Commissioner of the Chinese Imperial Maritime Customs, 1850–1951.

180 Raphoe Diocesan Archives/ Cartlann Ratha-Bhath

Address   The Bishop's House
              Letterkenny
              County Donegal

Telephone   (074) 36122/21208

Enquiries to   The Bishop's House

Opening hours   Postal enquiry only; photocopying
and facilities

Major collections
The archives, only recently established, is in the process of formation. It is
   essentially the episcopal archives, beginning with Bishop James
   McDevitt (1870–9). Papers of Bishops Daniel McGettigan, Michael
   Logue and Patrick O'Donnell are being acquired from Armagh Diocesan
   Archives (q.v.).

181 Redemptorist Fathers (Congregation of the Most Holy Redeemer)

Address   Liguori House
              75 Orwell Road
              Dublin 6

Telephone   (01) 492 2688

Enquiries to   The Archivist

Opening hours   By appointment; photocopying
and facilities

Major collections
Material relating to the history of Irish Redemptorists in Ireland, Australia,
   the Philippines, Brazil and India; to personnel; to the foundation and
   development of various Irish houses.
Material relating to apostolic works in Ireland including missions, the holy
   family confraternity and the Perpetual Novena to Our Lady of Perpetual
   Help.
Collections of sermons and of retreats to priests and religious; material
   relating to Irish retreat houses and new apostolates at home and abroad;
   house annals, 1851–.

182   Registry of Deeds

Address	Henrietta Street Dublin 1
Telephone	(01) 670 7500
Fax	(01) 804 8393
Enquiries to	The Senior Assistant Registrar
Opening hours and facilities	10.00–4.30, Mon–Fri; photocopying
Guides	Margaret Dickson Falley, *Irish and Scotch-Irish Ancestral Research* (2 vols.) P.B. Eustace (ed.), *Registry of Deeds, Abstract of wills* vol. i, *1708–45* (Dublin, 1956); do. vol. ii, *1746–85* (Dublin, 1954). Eilish Ellis & P.B. Eustace (eds), vol. iii, *1785–1832* (Dublin, 1984). Peter Roebuck, 'The Irish Registry of Deeds', *Irish Historical Studies* xviii, 69 (Mar 1972). P.B. Phair, 'Guide to the Registry of Deeds', *Analecta Hibernica* 23 (1966)

Major collections

Records of registered deeds of transfer of ownership or interest in property, 1708–, records of wills, 1708–1832. Some records of marriage settlements.

This office maintains an index of names of grantors, 1708–, and an index of placenames, 1708–1947, to all our records.

183   Religious Society of Friends Historical Library

Address	Swanbrook House Bloomfield Avenue Morehampton Road Donnybrook Dublin 4
Telephone	(01) 668 7157
Enquiries to	The Curator

Opening hours and facilities	11.00–1.00, Thur; photocopying
Guides	O.C. Goodbody *Guide to Irish Quaker Records, 1654–1860* (Dublin, 1967); P.B. Eustace & O.C. Goodbody *Abstracts of Wills and Inventories, 17th & 18th Century* (Dublin, 1957)

Major collections

Quaker records, minute books, family lists, sufferings.

Testimonies of denial, disownments, 17th–20th century.

Letters and documents relating to relief work in the Great Famine.

Registers of births, marriages and burials, 17th–20th century.

Collections of letters, 18th–20th century.

Diaries; records of Quaker schools in Ireland; collection of photograph albums and scrapbooks.

Museum items: samplers, embroidery, dress.

Pedigrees, wills, deeds, marriage certificates, 17th–20th century.

Pamphlets and correspondence related to Quaker mission and service.

184   Religious Society of Friends Ulster Quarterly Meeting

Address	Friends Meeting House 4 Magheralove Road Lisburn BT28 3BD County Antrim
Enquiries to	The Archives Committee
Opening hours and facilities	Postal enquiry only
Guides	O.C. Goodbody, *Guide to Irish Quaker Records, 1654–1860* (Dublin, 1967)

Major collections

Records of the Society of Friends in Ulster from 1673: minutes of meetings; births, marriages and death records; sufferings. These records are also available on microfilm in the Public Record Office of Northern Ireland (q.v.).

185   Representative Church Body Library

Address	Braemor Park Churchtown Dublin 14
Telephone	(01) 492 3979
Fax	(01) 492 4770
E-mail	library@ireland.anglican.org.
Website address	www.ireland.anglican.org
Enquiries to	The Librarian and Archivist
Opening hours and facilities	9.30–1.00, 1.45–5.00, Mon–Fri; photocopying; photography and microfilming by arrangement
Guides	J.B. Leslie, *Catalogue of manuscripts in possession of the Representative Church Body* (Dublin, 1938); Geraldine Fitzgerald, 'Manuscripts in the Representative Church Body Library', *Analecta Hibernica* 23 (1966); Raymond Refaussé 'The Representative Church Body Library and the Records of the Church of Ireland' in *Archivium Hibernicum* xlix, 1995; Raymond Refaussé, *Church of Ireland Records* (Dublin, 1999); Report of the Library and Archives Committee, containing an annual accessions list, is published annually in the *Journal of the General Synod of the Church of Ireland*; introductory leaflets.

Major collections

Church of Ireland archives mainly from the Republic of Ireland: records of over 650 parishes, mainly in Counties Carlow, Clare, Cork, Dublin, Galway, Kerry, Kildare, Kilkenny, Mayo, Meath, Westmeath and Wicklow, early 17th century–; records of 17 dioceses, especially Cloyne, Dublin, Glendalough & Kildare, Ossory, Ferns & Leighlin, Meath and Tuam, late 13th century–; records of 15 cathedrals, especially Christ Church and St Patrick's, Dublin, St Canice's, Kilkenny, and St Brigid's, Kildare, early 14th century–; records of the General Synod and the Representative Church Body, 1870–.

Records of societies and organizations related to the Church of Ireland: schools, educational societies, missionary organizations, clerical groups, 18th–20th century.

Miscellaneous ecclesiastical manuscripts: papers of bishops, clergy and laity, correspondence, diaries, research notes and writings, scrapbooks, photographs; transcripts of non–extant Church of Ireland records, 17th–20th century.

Microfilms of Church of Ireland records in other custodies, 17th–20th century.

Photographic archive mainly of church buildings but also of clergy, laity and church plate.

Oral history collection.

186 Rockwell College

Address	Cashel County Tipperary
Telephone	((062) 61444
Fax	((062) 61661
E-mail	rockwell@iol.ie
Website address	www.rockwell-college.ie
Enquiries to	The Archivist
Opening hours and facilities	By appointment only; letter of recommendation required; fee payable for research visit

Major collections

Records of students and staff of the College; photographs, 1864–; Rockwell Annual, 1926–; College and Community journals, 1864–.

Liturgical books: ceremonials and music books.

187 Roscommon County Council

Address	County Library Abbey Street Roscommon
Telephone	(0903) 37271/2/3/4/5/6/7
Fax	(0903) 25474
E-mail	roslib@iol.ie
Enquiries to	The County Librarian

Opening hours	1.00–8.00, Tue & Thur; 1.00–5.00, Wed; 10.00–1.00,
and facilities	2.00–5.00, Fri & Sat; prior notice recommended;
	photocopying

Major collections

Athlone: No. 2 Rural District Council minutes, 1899–1925.

Boyle: Board of Guardian minutes, 1883–1920; Dispensary District minutes, 1852–96; Rural District Council minutes, 1896–9, and quarterly minutes, 1900–25.

Carrick–on–Shannon: Rural District Council minutes, 1903–16.

Castlerea: Board of Guardian minutes, 1839–1908; Rural District Council minutes: 1902–25.

Roscommon: Board of Health minutes: 1921–42; County Council minutes: 1899–; Grand Jury records, 1818–99; Pension Committee minutes, 1908–51; Board of Guardian minutes, 1884–1921; Rural District Council minutes, 1899–1926; Town Commissioners minutes, 1873–1910.

Strokestown: Board of Guardian minutes, 1850–1913; Rural District Council minutes, 1899–1921.

Papers of the Lloyd family of Croghan, 1660–1935; papers of the Gately family.

188   Royal College of Physicians of Ireland

Address	6 Kildare Street
	Dublin 2
Telephone	(01) 661 6677
Fax	(01) 676 3989
Enquiries to	The Librarian
Opening hours	9.30–1.00, 2.00–5.00, Mon–Fri
and facilities	appointment advisable; photocopying
Guides	Brian Donnelly, 'Records of the Royal College of Physicians', *Irish Archives* 1 (1989)

Major collections

Complete series of College minute books, 1692–; registers of fellows and members, late 17th century–; Committee proceedings books, 1828–; College correspondence, 1863–; administrative records relating to the Library, 19th century.

Medical and Philosophical Society minutes, 1756–84, 1856–1939.

Dublin Sanitary Association minutes, late 19th century.

National Association for the Prevention of Tuberculosis minutes, late 19th century.

Cow Pock Institution subscription book, 1804–43.

Indian Hospital case books, late 19th century.

Westmoreland Lock Hospital records, 1792–1922.

Sir Dominick Corrigan (1802–80): private papers.

Kirkpatrick biographical file: information on some 10,000 Irish medical practitioners.

Sir Patrick Dun's Hospital records, 1808–1986; St Ultan's Hospital records, 1919–84.

189   Royal College of Surgeons in Ireland

Address	The Widdess Room (Archives & Rare Books) The Mercer Library Mercer Street Lower Dublin 2
Telephone	(01) 402 2439
Fax	(01) 402 2457
E-mail	archivist@ncsi.ie
Website address	www.rcsi.ie
Enquiries to	The Archivist
Opening hours and facilities	9.00–5.00, Mon–Fri; appointment advisable; photocopying; photography

Major collections

Records created by the Royal College of Surgeons in Ireland, 1784–.

Records created by other institutions. Mercer's Hospital (1734–1983): minute books of the governors 1736–; minute books of the medical board; clinical records of various departments of the hospital. House of Industry Hospitals: minute books of the Corporation for relieving the poor in the County and City of Dublin, 1772–1871. Meath Hospital (founded 1753): sixteen volumes including governors' minute books, 1807–. Surgical Society of Ireland (1833–83): minutes of meetings of Council.

Records created by individuals associated with the history of medicine in Ireland including Richard Butcher, surgeon to Mercer's Hospital, case books, 1846–59; Charles A. Cameron, College historian, diaries, 1880–1916; Abraham Colles (1773–1843), surgeon, documentation relating to Colles; James A. Deeny (1906–94), former Chief Medical Adviser to the Irish Government: papers; William Doolin (1887–1962), surgeon and literary figure: papers; A. Jacob, President RCSI, 1837 and 1864, correspondence, 1840–3; Patrick Logan MD (d.1988), chest physician and medical historian: papers; Bethel Solomons, gynaecologist: case books, 1914–21; L.B. Somerville-Large, ophthalmologist, case books, 1902–10; J.D.H. Widdess (1906–82), College librarian and historian, papers.

190   Royal Dublin Society

Address	Merrion Road Ballsbridge Dublin 4
Telephone	(01) 668 0866 ext.386
Fax	(01) 660 4014
Enquiries to	The Librarian
Opening hours and facilities	10.00–5.00, Tue, Fri; 10.00–7.00, Wed, Thur; by appointment; photocopying

Major collections

Original minute books, 1731–64 (proceedings published from the minutes after 1764); Science Committee minute books, 1816–1979; Library Committee minute books, 1816–1984; Industries, Art and General Purposes Committee minute books, 1890–1917; Fine Arts Committee minute books, 1816–89.

Private paper collections of Professor George Fitzgerald (School of Engineering, Trinity College, Dublin), Dr Horace H. Poole, Richard M. Barrington and John Edmund Carew.

Records of the Radium Institute.

Photographic collection.

191   Royal Irish Academy

Address	19 Dawson Street Dublin 2
Telephone	(01) 676 2570/676 4222

Fax	(01) 676 2346
E-mail	library@ria.ie
Website address	www.ria.ie
Enquiries to	The Librarian
Opening hours and facilities	10.30–5.30, Mon–Fri. The Library is closed for three weeks in August; non-members must present an application form signed by a member of the Academy or a letter of intoduction from a recognised institution; annual readers' tickets are issued for a fee of IR£10; photocopying and microfilm printouts; photography and microfilming by arrangement
Guides	*Catalogue of Irish Manuscripts in the Royal Irish Academy* (Dublin & London, 1926–70) 28 fascicules; Brigid Dolan 'Genealogical sources at the Royal Irish Academy' in *Aspects of Irish Genealogy* (Dublin, 1991); Elizabeth Fitzpatrick *The catalogue of Irish manuscripts in the Royal Irish Academy: a brief introduction* (Dublin, 1988)

Major collections

Over 30 manuscripts pre-1600 including the Cathach or Psalter of St Columba (6th century); Domhnach Airgid (8th century); Stowe Missal (9th century); Lebor na hUidre (12th century); Book of Ballymote (14th century); Austin Friars Breviary, Book of Fermoy, Book of Hours, Book of Lecan, Leabhar Breac (15th century).

Major collection of *c.*1,400 manuscripts in Irish, 17th–20th century, including the Hodges & Smith collection; the Betham, Hardiman, Hudson, O'Brien, O'Daly, O'Gorman and Reeves collections; the Stowe Irish manuscripts collection.

Antiquarian collections including the Hardiman and Windele papers; Ordnance Survey letters and memoirs; Gabriel Beranger watercolours; drawings of Dublin by George Petrie; topographical watercolours by Richard Colt Hoare; Ordnance Survey Sketches by George Victor du Noyer, George Petrie *et al.*; William Frederick Wakeman drawings.

Genealogical papers including those of Blackhall, De La Ponce, MacSwiney and Upton.

Natural history collections including those of A.H. Halliday, G.H. Kinahan, C. Longfield–Roberts, C.B. Moffatt, A.G. Moore, D.Y. Pack-Beresford, R.A. Phillips and R. Lloyd Praeger.

Papers of members of the R.I.A. including O.J. Bergin, R. Day, Lord Charlemont and E. Knott.

Papers and diaries including those of C. Gavan Duffy, Katherine and Martha Wilmot.

Muniments of the Royal Irish Academy from its foundation in 1785.

192   Royal Society of Antiquaries of Ireland

Address	63 Merrion Square, Dublin 2
Telephone	(01) 676 1749
Fax	(01) 676 1749
Enquiries to	The Librarian
Opening hours and facilities	2.00–5.00, Mon–Fri; by appointment; photocopying
Guides	William Cotter Stubbs, 'The Weavers' Guild, the Guild of the Blessed Virgin Mary, Dublin 1446–1840', *Journal of Royal Society of Antiquaries of Ireland* xliv, 1 (1919), 60–88

Major collections

Corporation books of Irish towns, especially from County Kilkenny; records of the Weavers' Guild of Dublin 1676–1840; archives of the RSAI, 1849–; a 13th century illuminated Sarum missal; topographical drawings including 12 volumes of sketches by George Victor du Noyer and one volume by George Miller; sketches of Dublin by Brian Coghlan; notebooks of Patrick Joseph O'Reilly (1854–1924), including transcripts of 1642 depositions, and 23 volumes of pedigrees of the O'Reilly's; papers of Francis Elrington Ball, 1863–1928, historian and antiquary; and the papers of Lord Walter Fitzgerald, 1858–1923, soldier and antiquary, founder and editor of the *County Kildare Archaeological Society Journal.*

193   Royal Ulster Rifles Regimental Museum

Address	RHQ The Royal Irish Rangers 5 Waring Street Belfast BT I 2EW
Telephone	(01232) 232086/247279

Enquiries to	The Honorary Curator
Opening hours and facilities	9.00–4.00, Mon–Fri

Major collections
Officers' records of service, 83rd and 86th regiments, 19th century (micro-film); recruits' registers, 1924–39; unit war diaries, World War I and World War II; medal rolls; photograph albums and scrapbooks, 1900–; films.

194   Sacred Heart Convent

Address	Society of the Sacred Heart of Jesus Mount Anville Road Dublin 14
Telephone	(01) 278 0610
Fax	(01) 278 2557
Enquiries to	The Archivist
Opening hours and facilities	10.00–12.00, 2.00–4.00, Tue–Thurs; appointment necessary; photocopying

Major collections
Congregational archives, 1800–, including material relating to the life, let-ters, spiritual and educational works of Sr Madeleine Sophie Barat, Janet Erskine Stuart and other educationalists of the congregation.
Material relating to schools of the congregation in Ireland, 1842–.

195   St Columb's Cathedral

Address	London Street Londonderry
Telephone	(01504) 267313
Enquiries to	The Tourist Guide
Opening hours and facilities	9.00–1.00, 2.00–4.00, Mon–Sat, winter; 9.00–5.00, Mon–Sat, summer

Major collections

Cathedral and parish records, 1642–.

Munn Collection: 32 volumes of copies of records relating to the history of the City and County of Londonderry, 17th–19th century.

Tenison Groves Collection: copies of records relating to Londonderry including valuable information on the history of the London Companies, 17th century–.

196   St Columba's College

Address	Rathfarnham Dublin 16
Telephone	(01) 490 6791
Fax	(010 493 6655
E-mail	tmacey@stcolumbas.ie *or* admin@stcolumbas.ie
Enquiries to	The Warden
Opening hours and facilities	By appointment

Major collections

Records relating to the administration of the College: College Register (record of entrances), 1843–, the year of foundation; minutes of the Fellows' meetings, 1890s–; minutes of Convention (staff meetings); accounts; pupils' reports.

Miscellaneous printed material relating to the foundation and history of the College including files of *The Columban,* 1879–, and the *Old Columban Bulletin, 1950–.*

Collection of photographs dating from 1859.

Founders' correspondence, 1841–2; letters from Dr J.H. Todd to Archbishop Lord John George Beresford, 1843; reminiscences of Revd William Sewell (1804–79), 1866.

Literary manuscripts; *The Lake Isle of Innisfree* presented by W.B. Yeats in 1936; *Museum by Æ* (George Russell); *In Exile* by Monk Gibbon; extract from A *Life* by Sir Dermot Boyle; two poems by Michael Ó Siadhail, 1991; and autographs of Douglas Hyde, Robin Flower and L.A.G. Strong.

A French Book of Hours, mid–14th century.

Correspondence relating to the Mioseach, a medieval Irish book shrine, 1843–.

197 St Columban's Missionary Society

Address	St Columban's Grange Road Donaghmede Dublin 13
Telephone	(01) 847 6647
Fax	(01) 848 4025
Enquiries to	The Archivist
Opening hours and facilities	10.00–5.00, Mon–Fri; by appointment; photocopying

Major collections
Correspondence relating to the foundation and development of the Society
in China and the other countries where it is represented, 1912–.

198 St Finian's College

Address	Mullingar County Westmeath
Telephone	(044) 48672
Fax	(044) 45275
Enquiries to	The President
Opening hours and facilities	By appointment; photocopying

Major collections
College papers: accounts, student lists, examination results, photographs,
19th–20th century.
Papers of Fr John Brady, diocesan historian, 1930s–60s; papers of Fr
Michael McManus, mostly relating to the 1798 Rebellion in Counties
Meath, Westmeath and Kildare, 1920s–70s.

199 St Kieran's College, Kilkenny

Address	St Kieran's College Kilkenny

Telephone	(056) 21086
Fax	(056) 70001
Enquiries to	The Archivist
Opening hours and facilities	By appointment; photocopying

Major collections

Carrigan and Graves MSS; collections of local interest compiled by priests of the diocese including Fr Moore, Healy, Clohessy and Dowling.

Research notes on College history; College account books, 1811–; index of students, 1782–1950; photographs and maps.

200 St Louis' Sisters

Address	St Louis' Convent Monaghan County Monaghan
Telephone	(047) 81411/83076
Enquiries to	The Archivist
Opening hours and facilities	Archives available by appointment; Heritage Centre open 10.00–12.00, 2.00–4.00, Mon–Sat; 2.00–4.00, Sun; closed Wed

Major collections

Material relating to the history of the congregation including annals, minutes, account books, legal documents and building records. Photographic and three dimensionsal collections held in the Heritage Centre.

201 St Malachy's College, Belfast

Address	36 Antrim Road Belfast BT15 2AE
Telephone	(01232) 74828
Enquiries to	The Archivist
Opening hours and facilities	By appointment; photocopying

Major collections
Archives of the College including lists of former students, *c.*1856–1926; account books, *c.*1844–; memoirs, diaries and photographs.

O'Laverty MSS: 16 Gaelic manuscripts acquired by Monsignor James O'Laverty P.P., Holywood, County Down (d. 1906), historian of the Diocese of Down and Connor, also available on microfilm in the National Library (q.v.).

Donnellan MSS: 2 Gaelic manuscripts from the South Armagh/North Louth region, collected by Revd L. Donnellan P.P., County Armagh.

Correspondence of Muiris Ó Droighneain, Gaelic scholar and former head of Irish at St Malachy's, relating mainly to literary matters, *c.*1930–65. Cuttings of books and fragmentary notes of Laurence O'Neill, Lord Mayor of Dublin, *c.*1918–24.

202 St Patrick's College, Carlow

Address	St Patrick's College Carlow
Telephone	(0503) 31114
Fax	(0503) 40258
E-mail	stafspcc@rtc-carlow.ie
Website address	www.carlowcollege.ie
Enquiries to	The Archivist
Opening hours and facilities	By appointment only; photocopying

Major collections
The archives house part of the College Library collection, particularly materials relating to Bishops of Kildare and Leighlin, to diocesan history, and to notable past students of Carlow College.

Microfilmed account books can be consulted at the National Library, Dublin (q.v.); this is the main source on early students of the College, 1793–.

203 St Patrick's College, Cavan

Address	The Bishop's Residence Cullies Cavan
Telephone	(049) 433 1496

| *Enquiries to* | The Archivist |
| *Opening houry and facilities* | By appointment |

Major collections

Archives of the College including rolls, prize lists, deeds, plans and account books, 1839–.

204   St Patrick's College of Education

Address	Drumcondra Dublin 9
Telephone	(01) 837 6191
Fax	(01) 837 6197
Enquiries to	The Chairperson, Archives Committee
Opening hours and facilities	Access restricted until material has been processed; photocopying

Major collections

Archives of the College as an institution for the training of primary teachers. The material, which is not extensive, has only recently been centrally located and is now being processed.

205   St Patrick's College, Maynooth

Address	Maynooth County Kildare
Telephone	(01) 628 5222
Fax	(01) 628 9063
Enquiries to	The College Archivist or Librarian, Russell Library
Opening hours and facilities	10.00–1.00, 2.00–5.00 Mon–Thurs; by appointment; photocopying, photography, microfilm

Major collections

Archives of the College, 1795–.

Archives of the Irish College at Salamanca and other Irish colleges in Spain; *c.*50,000 documents, 1592–1936.

St Patrick's College, Maynooth *see also* National University of Ireland, Maynooth

206 St Patrick's College, Thurles

Address	Thurles County Tipperary
Telephone	(0504) 21201/24466
Fax	(0504) 23735
E-mail	luceaet@tinet.ie
Enquiries to	The Archivist
Opening hours and facilities	By appointment; photocopying

Major collections

Much of the College archives relates to College administration since its foundation in 1837 and is pastorally privileged, confidential and inaccessible. Basic biographical information on past students is available as well as considerable material on day to day expenses and property.

Papers of Fr Michael Maher containing biographical material on former clergy of the archdiocese of Cashel and Emly and material relevant to parochial histories of the archdiocese. Includes a diary commenting upon contemporary ecclesiastical and civil events with particular reference to the War of Independence.

Parochial register for the parish of Boherlahan, 1736–40.

207 St Patrick's Hospital

Address	Steeven's Lane James's Street Dublin 8
Telephone	(01) 677 5423
Enquiries to	The Chief Executive Officer/Medical Director
Opening hours and facilities	By appointment only

Major collections

Records from the foundation of the hospital in 1745 up to the present day including the following:

Records relating to the general administration of the hospital. Among the most significant of these are a complete set of minute book of the Board of Governors from the foundation of the hospital; foundation charter and subsequent supplemental charters; reports of government inspectors on the hospital from the late 19th and early 20th centuries; records relating to some of the masters or medical superintendents of the hospital, especially Dr Richard Leeper (medical superintendent, 1899–1942).

Records relating to the hospital's finances and property including petitions to parliament for funding, 1755 & 1757; patient accounts, late 19th century; maps, correspondence, rentals and legal records relating to estates owned by the hospital in Dublin, Ferns and Saggart, mid-18th century–.

Records relating to patients including admission records, 1841–; registers of patients, 1795–; medical records, 1845–; reports and statistical information on patients, mainly 20th century.

Financial and legal papers concerning the final years of Jonathan Swift and the administration of his estate in relation to the foundation of the hospital including records of the committee of guardians appointed to administer Swift's affairs in the last years of his life; records relating to Swift's funeral; records created by the trustees appointed under the terms of Swift's will to found the hospital.

Records relating to the hospital buildings including the original plans and specifications for the building by the architect, George Semple, 1749; plans of later additions and refurbishments; plans for a district lunatic asylum submitted to the hospital by the architect, Francis Johnston.

Records documenting the history of St Edmundsbury, a convalescent branch of the hospital which was established in Lucan in 1899, including a survey of the estate of Agmondisham Vesey of 1772 incorporating a survey of the St Edmundsbury estate.

208 St Peter's College

Address	Summerhill
	Wexford
Telephone	(053) 45111/42071
Fax	(053) 45111
E-mail	president@stpeterscollege.iol.ie

Enquiries to	The President
Opening hours and facilities	By appointment; photocopying

Major collections
Hore Manuscripts relating to the history of Wexford, *c.*1798.
Material relating to the development of St Peter's College, 1811–.
Material relating to the diocese of Ferns.
Papers of Revd T. O'Byrne, G. Flood and R. Ranson.

209 Servite Fathers (Order of Friar Servants of Mary)

Address	Servite Priory Benburb Dungannon County Tyrone
Telephone	(01861) 548241
Enquiries to	The Archivist, Servite Priory, Grange Wood, Rath-farnham, Dublin 16. Telephone (01) 932913/932073
Opening hours and facilities	Postal enquiry; photocopying

Major collections
Material relating mainly to the Order in Ireland including the foundation
  years, 1947–, with some material relating to the Order worldwide.

210 Sisters of Charity

Address	Religious Sisters of Charity Generalate CARITAS 15, Gilford Road Sandymount Dublin 4
Telephone	(01) 269 7833

Fax	(01) 260 3085
Enquiries to	The Archivist
Opening hours and facilities	9.00–12.30, 2.00–5.00, Mon–Thurs; 9.00–12.30, Fri; appointment and letter of recommendation for first time researchers required; photocopying

Major collections

Material relating to the life and work of the Sisters of Charity from their foundation in 1815. The largest collections relates to the foundress, Mary Aikenhead, and there is also a substantial body of material relating to Mother Arsenius Morrough-Bernard and the Providence Woollen Mills which she established in Foxford, County Mayo, to provide employment for local people.

211   Sisters of Mercy

Address	Mercy Central Archive 23 Herbert Street Dublin 2
Telephone	(01) 638 7521
Fax	(01) 638 7523
Enquiries to	The Archivist
Opening hours and facilities	By appointment only; photocopying

Major collections

Archives of the Sisters of Mercy in the diocese of Dublin, 1880–1950, including rules and constitutions, customs and minor regulations; meditations for retreats; reception and profession ceremonials; prayer books; correspondence; administrative papers, papers relating to converts in the diocese and foundations abroad; papers relating to the promotion of the Cause of Catherine McAuley.

Archives of Our Lady of Mercy Teacher Training College, Carysfort, Blackrock, County Dublin, 1883–1955, including administrative papers; architectural plans; reports of the Commissioners of National Education, 1883–1920; reports of the Department of Education, 1924–33; report and programme presented by the national programme conference to the Minister of Education, 1925–6; programmes of examinations for entrance to the training college and for students in training, 1933–44; college concert programmes; matriculation for the National University of Ireland, 1952; correspondence with the Office of National Education, 1900–15; correspondence with the Department of Education, 1922–40; rules and programmes for secondary schools, 1931–49; programmes of primary instruction, 1926–48; rules for national schools, 1934; notes for national teachers issued by the Department of Education, 1933–52; correspondence with the Archbishop of Dublin, 1900–20; golden jubilee celebrations, 1952; *Child Education* periodicals, 1924; instrumental and vocal scores; articles on Irish educational theory and history; primary school readers.

Archives of St Brigid's Convent, Naas, County Kildare, 1860–1950, including administrative papers; rules and constitutions; customs and minor regulations; reception and profession ceremonials; hymnals; spiritual reflections.

Archives of St John's Convent of Mercy, Birr, County Offaly, 1838–1957, including specifications for the convent by E.W. Pugin, 1838; architectural plans by Pugin and Ashlin, 1855; general specifications and architectural plans, 1909–37; press cuttings; Lenten pastorals of the Bishop of Killaloe, 1937–57; letters from the Bishop of Killaloe, 1866–1939; meditations and considerations for retreats; rules and constitutions; honorariums; correspondence, 1847–92; decrees and rulings of the Sacred Congregation for Religious and Secular Institutes, 1926–52; letters regarding the cause of Catherine McAuley, 1937–8; notes on the Crotty shrine; history of the convent.

Archives of St Michael's Convent of Mercy, Athy, County Kildare, 1852–1954, including copy letter books of Mother Teresa Maher, 1861–90; novitiate registers, 1855–99; account books, 1855–97; minute book of the Children of Mary, 1875-6; architectural plans, 1892–1902; papers relating to a foundation in Brisbane, Australia, 1862–9; administrative papers; rules and constitutions.

Archives of Coláiste Íde Preparatory School, Dingle, County Kerry, 1928–55; St Catherine's Convent of Mercy, Baggot Street, Dublin, 1870–1950; St Mary's Convent of Mercy, Arklow, County Wicklow, 1876–1950; Convent of Mercy, Borrisokane, County Tipperary, 1900–52; St Michael's Convent of Mercy, Newtownforbes, County Longford, 1869–1950.

Archives of some thirty two industrial schools, residential homes and orphanges run by the Sisters of Mercy. Former residents of the schools and homes may obtain information about their placement by writing to the archives. Access by third parties is restricted under the 100 year rule. The institutions include the following:

149

Antrim: St Patrick's, Crumlin Road, Belfast, 1869–1920; Whiteabbey, Belfast, 1894–1912.

Clare: St Xavier's, Ennis, 1880–1963; Kilrush, 1870–1956.

Cork: Wellington Road, Cork, 1877–1886; St Aloysius, Clonakilty, 1869–1974; Our Lady of Mercy, Kinsale, 1869–1987; St Colman's, Rushbrook, Cobh, 1870–1987; St Joseph's, Mallow, 1880–1972; St Joseph's, Passage West, 1882–1986.

Dublin: St Anne's, Booterstown, 1870–1972; St Vincent's, Goldenbridge, 1880–1985.

Galway: St Joseph's, Clifden, 1872–1971; St Bridget's, Loughrea, 1869–1963; St Joseph's, Ballinasloe, 1884–1964; St Anne's, Renmore, Lenaboy, 1869–1966.

Kerry: St Joseph's, Killarney, 1869–1986; Pembroke Alms House/ Nazareth, Tralee, 1895–1988.

Louth: St Joseph's, Dundalk, 1881–1971.

Limerick: St Vincent's, Limerick, 1846–1979.

Longford: Our Lady of Succour, Newtownforbes, 1870–1964.

Mayo: St Columba's, Westport, 1871–1962.

Offaly: St John's, Birr, 1870–1959.

Sligo: St Laurence's, Sligo, 1908–44.

Tipperary: Nenagh, 1900–16; St Augustine's, Templemore, 1870–1964.

Tyrone: St Catherine's, Strabane, 1879–1948.

Waterford: St Michael's, Cappoquin, 1873–1987.

Westmeath: Mount Carmel, Moate, 1870–1978; St Joseph's, Summerhill, 1904–64.

Wexford: St Michael's, Wexford, 1869–1971.

Wicklow: St Kyran's, Rathdrum, 1884–1986.

212   Sisters of St Claire

Address	91 Harold's Cross Road Dublin 6W
Enquiries to	The Archivist
Opening hours and facilities	Postal enquiries only

Major collections

Material relating to the history of the Order, and work, since 1629, in Ireland.

213 Sisters of St Claire

Address   High Street
                  Newry
                  County Down

Enquiries to   The Archivist

Opening hours   Postal enquiries only
and facilities

Major collections
Material relating to the history of the Order, and work, since 1629, in
  Ireland.

214 Sligo Corporation

Address   Market Yard
                  Sligo

Telephone   (071) 47714/47718

Enquiries to   The Town Clerk

Opening hours   9.00–1.00, 2.00–5.00, Mon–Fri
and facilities

Major collections
Minutes of Sligo Corporation meetings, 1842–1991; register of premises
  (Explosives Act, 1875), 1879–1916; register of music performed in the
  Town Hall, 1938–46; register of public entertainments (Town Hall),
  1930–48; minutes of artisans & housing committees, 1886–1920; lists of
  burgesses of Sligo Borough, 1868–1906; Sligo Cemetery Trust ledger,
  1868–86; valuation & rate books, 1842–.

215 Sligo County Library

Address   Sligo County Library Headquarters
                  The Westward Town Centre
                  Bridge Street
                  Sligo

Telephone   (071) 47190

151

Fax	(071) 46798
E-mail	sligolib@iol.ie
Enquiries to	The County Librarian
Opening hours and facilities	10.00–12.54, 2.00–4.45 Mon–Fri; photocopying
Guides	*Sligo: Sources of Local History* (1988)

Major collections

Minute books of Board of Guardians, 1850–90; Grand Jury Presentments minute books, 1813–51 & 1877–99; Sligo County Council minute books, 1899–1950.

J.C. McDonagh MSS relating to County Sligo (22 vols).

Rentals of Palmerston Estate, 1860, 1879, 1888, 1902.

Pedigrees of various county families.

Drawings of antiquities of County Sligo by W.F. Wakeman.

216   Sligo Harbour Commissioners

Address	Harbour Office Custom House Quay Sligo
Telephone	(071) 61197
Fax	(071) 61197
Enquiries to	The Secretary
Opening hours and facilities	9.00–5.00, Mon–Fri

Major collections

Minute books, 1824–8, 1847–; memoranda of agreements book, 1823–92; miscellaneous accounts and operational books, late 19th century–; report on improvements to harbour, 1822.

217   Society of African Missions

Address	Blackrock Road Cork
Telephone	(021) 292871

Fax	(021) 293876
Enquiries to	The Archivist
Opening hours and facilities	By appointment

Major collections
Correspondence and papers of the Irish Province of the Society from 1885 to the present day including material relating to the administration of the Irish Houses of the Province and the Province's Missions in Liberia, Nigeria, Tanzania, Zambia, South Africa, Australia and South America: coutumiers, diaries and memoirs; material on the individual jurisdictions staffed by the Society; biographical material on members of the Province.

218   Society of St Vincent de Paul

Address	8 New Cabra Road Dublin 7
Telephone	(01) 838 4164/7
Fax	(01) 838 7355
Enquiries to	The National Secretary
Opening hours and facilities	9.30–5.30, Mon–Fri, by appointment

Major collections
Records of the Society, 1833–; material relating to the founder, Frederic Ozanam, and to St Vincent de Paul; copies of the Society's *Bulletin*.

219   South Eastern Education and Library Board

Address	Library Headquarters Windmill Hill Ballynahinch County Down BT24 8DH
Telephone	(01232) 566400
Fax	(01232) 565072

E-mail	ref@bhinchlibhq.demon.uk
Enquiries to	The Principal Assistant Librarian, Irish and Local Studies
Opening hours and facilities	9.00–5.15, Mon–Fri; telephone in advance for an appointment if possible

Major collections
Material relating to travel and literature in County Down.
Collections of photographs and postcards.

220 Southern Education and Library Board

Address	Library Headquarters 1 Markethill Road Armagh BT60 1NR
Telephone	(01861) 525353
Fax	(01861) 526879
Enquiries to	The Irish and Local Studies Librarian
Opening hours and facilities	9.30–5.00, Mon, Thurs, and Fri; 9.30–7.15, Tue and Wed; photocopying

Major collections
Croslé papers relating to the history of Newry and district.
Southern Education and Library Board annual reports and minutes, 1973–.
Armagh, Banbridge, Cookstown and Newry Board of Guardians minutes (microfilm).

221 Stranmillis University College: a College of The Queen's University of Belfast

Address	Stranmillis Road Belfast BT9 5DY
Telephone	(01232) 384310
Fax	(01232) 663682
E-mail	Library@Stran-ni.ac.uk

Enquiries to   The Librarian

Opening hours   Term, 9.00–9.00, Mon–Thurs; 9.00–4.30, Fri;
and facilities   vacation, 9.00–5.00, Mon–Thurs; 9.00–4.30, Fri;
photocopying

Major collections
Documentary and photographic records of the College and grounds since
its establishment in 1922. Also prospectuses and other printed ephemera.

222   Temple House

Address   Ballymote
County Sligo

Telephone   (071) 83329

Fax   (071) 83808

E-mail   guests@templehouse.ie

Website   www.templehouse.ie/

Enquiries to   The Proprietor

Opening hours   By appointment
and facilities

Major collections
Papers of the Percival family and of the related Metcalfe, Bayley, de
Hammel and Blane families, mostly 1864–.

223   Tipperary Joint Libraries

Address   Castle Avenue
Thurles
County Tipperary

Telephone   (0504) 21555/21154/21102/21156

Fax   (0504) 23442

E-mail   studies@tipplibs.iol.ie

Website address   www.iol.ie/stipplibs

Enquiries to	Local Studies Department
Opening hours and facilities	10.00–1.00, 2.00–5.30, Mon–Fri; photocopying
Guides	Introductory leaflet available in branch libraries

Major collections

Poor Law Union records: Borrisokane, 1850–1925; Cashel, 1844–1925; Clogheen, 1839–1929; Clonmel, 1839–1924; Nenagh, 1839–1924; Roscrea, 1839–1924; Thurles, 1839–1924; Tipperary, 1839–1923.

Presentments to the Grand Juries of Tipperary, 1842–99.

Rentals, maps, schedules relating to the sale of encumbered estates: lands in the barony of Slieveardagh/Comsy, 1851; estates of the Earl of Portarlington at Borrisoleigh, 1855 and Roscrea, 1858; estate of Viscount Chabot at Thurles and Thomastown, 1859.

Family papers: Coopers of Killenure, 1879–98; Ryans of Inch, 1650–1928.

224   Tipperary South Riding County Museum

Address	Parnell Street Clonmel
Telephone	(052) 25399 (ext. 371)
Fax	(052) 24355
Enquiries to	The Curator
Opening hours and facilities	10.00–1.00, 2.00–5.00, Tue–Sat; by appointment; photocopying
Guides	An introductory leaflet and a series of interpretative lists and hand lists are available

Major collections

The County Museum holds an amount of archival material relating to local authorities in the county. It includes the minute books of Tipperary S.R. County Council, 1899–1952, and of various Council committees as well as the minute books of Fethard Town Commissioners, 1866–77, 1896–1929. The collections also include material relating to the Lismore estate and the records of the Republican Courts in the eastern part of the county during the War of Independence, for which three days notice is required.

225

Trinity College, Dublin
Geological Museum

Address

Geological Museum
Department of Geology
Trinity College
Dublin 2

Telephone　(01) 608 1477

Fax　(01) 671 1199

E-mail　wysjcknp@tcd.ie

Enquiries to　The Curator

Opening hours　10.00–4.30, Mon–Fri; groups by appointment;
and facilities　photocopying; photography

Guides　P.N. Wyse Jackson, 'Museum File 18: Geological
Museum, Trinity College, Dublin', *Geology Today* 6
(1989), 213–4; P.N. Wyse Jackson, 'The Geological
Collections of Trinity College, Dublin', *The
Geological Curator* 5, 7 (1992), 263–74.

Major collections

Charlesworth, Edward (1813–93): catalogue of specimens sent to Professor
Oldham *c.*1848.

Geological Society of Dublin/Royal Geological Society of Ireland: Minute
books and other manuscript items (detailed by Davies 1965). Graydon,
Revd George (d. 1803), cleric: diary of travels in Northern Italy (*c.*1792);
catalogue of volcanic products collected in Italy. Griffith, Sir Richard
(1784–1878), geologist and public servant: manuscript catalogue of car-
boniferous fossils presented to the Dublin University Museum (1844).

Hudson, R.G.S. (1895–1965), geologist: correspondence. Joly, John
(1857–1933), geologist: diaries, manuscripts, research notebooks, and
catalogue of mineral collection.

Knox, Hon. George (1765–1827), Parliamentarian: three catalogues of
minerals, some of which are now in TCD.

Leskean collection: manuscript entitled 'Synopsis of the arrangement of
the Vulcanic Cabinet annexed to the Leskean Collection in the Museum
of the Dublin Society', written on paper, watermark dated 1804. This collection was acquired by the Dublin Society in 1792 and is now in the
National Museum of Ireland.

Mallett, Robert (1810–81), civil engineer, seismologist: catalogue of volcanic products collected in Italy in 1864 and 1869.

Perceval, Robert: Professor of Chemistry, TCD: catalogue of minerals *(c.* 1803).

Ryan, James: Geological report on Isabella Pit, Workington (*c.*1798).

Smyth, Louis Bouvier (1893–1953), geologist: correspondence, laboratory notebooks, field notebooks, field maps.

Sollas, William Johnson (1849–1936), geologist: letter relating to Piltdown Man.

226   Trinity College Library, Dublin Manuscripts Department

Address	College Street Dublin 2
Telephone	(01) 608 1189
Fax	(01) 608 2690
E-mail	mscripts@tcd.ie
Website address	www.tcd.ie/Library/
Enquiries to	The Keeper of Manuscripts
Opening hours and facilities	10.00–5.00, Mon–Fri, I0.00–1.00, Sat; photography; microfilming
Guides	T. K. Abbott, *Catalogue of the Manuscripts in the Library of Trinity College, Dublin* (Dublin and London, 1900) is a general catalogue of accessions to 1900, continued after that date in typescript form. Introductory leaflet to the department is available throughout the Library. Sectional language catalogues have appeared in print, including T.K. Abbott and E.J. Gwynn, *Catalogue of the Irish Manuscripts in the Library of Trinity College, Dublin* (Dublin, 1921); Marvin L. Colker, A *Descriptive Catalogue of the Mediaeval and Renaissance Latin Manuscripts in the Library of Trinity College Dublin* (Scolar Press for Trinity College Library Dublin, 1991). Peter Fox (ed.), *Treasures of the Library, Trinity College Dublin* (Dublin, 1986) discusses some of the major holdings.

Major collections

Corpus of medieval manuscripts, largely from the collection of James

Ussher (d.1656), but also including the Library's greatest treasures: the Book of Kells (*c*.800), Book of Durrow (*c*.675), Book of Armagh (807), Book of Dimma (8th century), Book of Mulling (8th century), Matthew Paris's life of St Alban (13th century), Fagel Missal (15th century).

College muniments, 16th–20th century; Roman inquisitorial records, 16th–18th century; Depositions of 1641; 1798 rebellion papers; archives of the Royal Zoological Society of Ireland, 1836–*c*.1953.

Family and private paper collections of William King (1650–1729), archbishop of Dublin; Thomas Parnell (1679–1718), poet; Earls of Donoughmore, 16th–20th century; Wynne family of Hazlewood, County Sligo and Glendalough, County Wicklow, 18th–20th century; Elvery family of Carrickmines and Foxrock, County Dublin, 19th–20th century; Sir William Rowan Hamilton (1805–65), mathematician and astronomer; Michael Davitt (1846–1906), author and politician; John Dillon (1851–1927), politician; Robert Erskine Childers (1870–1922), author and politician; Liam de Róiste (1882–1959), politician and author; John Millington Synge (1871–1909), poet and dramatist; Susan Mitchell (1866–1926), poet and editor; Thomas Bodkin (1887–1961), art historian and gallery director; Thomas MacGreevy (1893–1967), poet and gallery director; Denis Johnston (1901–84), playwright and journalist; Frank Gallagher (1893–1962), journalist; Joseph Campbell (1876–1944), poet; James Stephens (1880–1950), author; Martin Ó Cadhain (1905–70), writer in Irish; George McBeth (1932–93), poet and novelist; John Banville (born 1945), novelist; Samuel Beckett (1906–89), author; Hubert Butler (1900–90), essayist; Gerald Barry (born 1952), composer; John B. Keane (born 1928), author.

227   Ulster Folk and Transport Museum Library

Address	Cultra Manor Holywood County Down BT18 0EU
Telephone	(01232) 428428
Fax	(01232) 428728
Enquiries to	The Librarian
Opening hours and facilities	9.00–5.00, Mon–Fri; photocopying; photography
Guides	M. McCavana and G. Loughran, *The B.B.C. Radio Archive Catalogue for Northern Ireland (1992)*

Major collections

Byers folklore collection, *c.*1900; Committee on Ulster Folklife and Traditions notebooks, *c.*1960; Huddleston vernacular poetry collection, *c.*1830–80; Ulster Dialect Dictionary collection.

W.A. Green photographic collection; Harland & Wolff photographic collection.

British Broadcasting Corporation archive: radio programmes since the inception of the B.B.C. in Northern Ireland in 1924 but most of the material is from the 1960s onwards; film archive from the 1950s but mostly from the 1960s.

228   Ulster Museum

Address	Botanic Gardens Belfast BT9 5AB
Telephone	(01232) 383000
Fax	(01232) 383003
Enquiries to	The Department of History
Opening hours and facilities	10.00–12.30, 2.00–4.30, Mon–Fri; prior appointment preferred; photocopying; photography
Guides	*Concise catalogue of the drawings, paintings & sculptures in the Ulster Museum* (Ulster Museum, 1986); N. Fisher, 'George Crawford Hyndman's MSS', *Journal of Conchology* xix (1931), 164; B.S. Turner and others, *A List of the Photographs in the R.J. Welch Collection in the Ulster Museum*, 1: *Topography and History* (Ulster Museum, 1979); 2: *Botany, Geology and Zoology* (Ulster Museum, 1983).

Major collections

Templeton MSS: *c.*25 vols of MSS of John Templeton (1766–1825), botanist; including his journal, 1806–25, several volumes of an unpublished Irish flora illustrated by himself, records of mosses and ferns and a list of Irish shells.

Hyndman MSS: numerous notes by George C. Hyndman (1796–1868), Belfast marine biologist; also dredging papers, Belfast Bay, 1844–57.

Thompson MSS: several folders of notes and correspondence of William Thompson (1805–52), Belfast naturalist and author of *Natural History of Ireland.*

Welch MSS: *c.*20 vols of personal and excursion diaries, natural history notes, memoranda and lists of negatives of Robert J. Welch (1859–1936), photographer and amateur naturalist.

Botany and Zoology Department: small but important collections, including notebooks of P.H. Grierson (1859–1952) on Mollusca and one letter of Dr Alexander Henry Halliday (?1728–1802) relating to Insecta.

Local History Department: extensive archive of manuscript and printed material, including the Barber MSS (Revd Samuel Barber of Rathfriland, United Irishman) and the Tennant Collection (Robert J. Tennant, early 19th century Liberal politician from Belfast).

Non–manuscript material: posters and other ephemera, chiefly playbills and programmes of Belfast theatres (*c.*200–250 items).

Belfast and other locally printed books, pamphlets, chapbooks and broadsides (*c.*500 items).

Hogg Collection: approx. 5,500 glass plate negatives plus many lantern slides, by A.R. Hogg of Belfast (1870–1939), covering topography, industry, commerce, social conditions and portraits.

Welch Collection: *c.*6,000 glass plate negatives by R.J. Welch of Irish subjects, covering topography, industries, rural crafts, antiquities, geology, botany and zoology.

Historical and Topographic Collection: *c.*1,000 negatives, modern and copied from old prints and negatives (constantly growing); a few other collections, large and medium-sized (uncatalogued or in process of being catalogued).

A growing collection of several hundred slides made in the field and from specimens and photographs.

Departments other than Local History keep their own specialized collections of negatives and slides.

Local History Department: *c.*250 maps; *c.*1,500 topographical drawings, paintings and prints; *c.*250 portraits.

Art Department: *c.*2,000 drawings and watercolors.

Botany and Zoology Department: various watercolours and drawings.

229   Ulster Television Film Library

Address	Havelock House
	Ormeau Road
	Belfast BT7 1EB
Telephone	(01232) 328122
Fax	(01232) 246695
Enquiries to	Film Librarian
Opening hours	By appointment or postal enquiry

Major collections
Most programmes produced by Ulster Television, 1957–.
Film and VTR record of most major events in Northern Ireland, 1957–.

230 Unitarian Church

Address	112 St Stephen's Green Dublin 2
Enquiries to	The Secretary
Opening hours and facilities	By appointment only

Major collections
Records of Eustace Street (formerly New Row), Cook Street and St Stephen's Green, (formerly Wood Street), Dublin, congregations, early 18th century–.
Records of Cork (Princes Street) congregation, 1799–1844.
Irish Unitarian Christian Society: minutes, 1830–99.

University College Cork *see* National University of Ireland, Cork

231 University College Dublin Archives Department

Address	Belfield Dublin 4
Telephone	(01) 706 7547
Fax	(01) 706 1146
E-mail	seamus.helferty@ucd.ie
Website address	www.ucd.ie/~archives
Enquiries to	The Archivist
Opening hours and facilities	10.00–1.00, 2.00–5.00, Mon–Thurs; 10.00–1.00, 2.00–4.00, Fri; reader's ticket and appointment necessary; photocopying; photography; digitisation

Major collections

Private paper collections relating to the movement for national independence and the history and development of the modern Irish state. Major collections include the papers of Frank Aiken, Todd Andrews, Kevin Barry, Ernest Blythe, Colonel Dan Bryan, Michael Collins, the Cumann na nGaedheal and Fine Gael parties, Desmond FitzGerald, Michael Hayes, T.M. Healy, Sighle Humphreys, Hugh Kennedy, Tom Kettle, Seán MacEntee, Seán MacEoin, Patrick McGilligan, Eoin MacNeill, Mary MacSwiney, Terence MacSwiney, Richard Mulcahy, Donnchadh Ó Briain, Daniel O'Connell, Kathleen O'Connell, Cearbhall Ó Dálaigh, Diarmuid Ó hÉigeartaigh, Ernie O'Malley, The O'Rahilly, Desmond Ryan, Dr James Ryan, Moss Twomey and Eamon de Valera.

Family and estate paper collections, 17th century–, of the Bryan family (Dublin); Caulfield (Tyrone); de Clifford (Down); Delachirois (Down); Fitzpatrick (Laois); Hart-Synnot (Dublin); Herbert (Kerry); Hutchinson and Synge Hutchinson (Dublin and Wicklow); Potter (Down); Rice of Mountrice (Kildare); Upton (Westmeath and Louth); and Wandesford (Kilkenny).

Trade union archives and labour–related private paper collections, deposited through the Irish Labour History Society (q.v.). Includes archives of actors, bakers, coopers, municipal employees, plasterers, shoe and leather workers, and woodworkers trade unions.

232 University College Dublin College Archives

Address	Archives Department Belfield Dublin 4
Telephone	(01) 706 7553
Fax	(01) 706 1146
E-mail	rena.lohan@ucd.ie
Website	www.ucd.ie/~archives
Enquiries to	The College Archivist
Opening hours and facilities	10.00–1.00, 2.00–5.00, Mon–Thur; 10.00–1.00, 2.00–4.00, Fri; reader's ticket and appointment necessary; photocopying, photography, digitisation

Major collections

Records of the Governing Body and its committees; of the administrative offices of the President, Registrar, Secretary and Bursar; of the Academic Council; and of faculties and their respective departments.

Video recordings with former officers and staff of the College.

Records documenting the wider College community, including student, staff and alumni societies and associations, such as the Literary and Historical Society, Academic Staff Association and the National University Women Graduates' Association.

Records of predecessor institutions: the Catholic University of Ireland, 1854–1911; Royal College of Science for Ireland, 1867–1926; Museum of Irish Industry, 1846–47; Albert Agricultural College, 1838–1926; and the Royal Veterinary College of Ireland, 1900–60.

233 University College Dublin Roinn Bhéaloideas Éireann/ Department of Irish Folklore

Address	Belfield Dublin 4
Telephone	(01) 706 8216/706 8327
Fax	(01) 706 1144
E-mail	hennigan@macollamh.ucd.ie
Enquiries to	Head of Department
Opening hours and facilities	2.30–5.30, Mon–Fri, excluding August; the Irish Folk Music section of the Department (UCD, Earlsfort Terrace) is open by appointment; photocopying; photography; microfilming
Guides	Seán O Súilleabháin, A *Handbook of Irish Folklore* (Dublin, 1942 and Detroit, 1970)

Major collections

Manuscripts, films, photographs, drawings and sound recordings held by the former Irish Folklore Commission (1935–71) as well as substantial additions, including video recordings, to these collections since 1971. The bulk of the manuscript holdings and sound and video recordings is in the Irish language, but these collections also contain large amounts of English-language material as well as smaller amounts of material in Scottish Gaelic and in the Manx and Breton languages.

234 University College Dublin Special Collections

Address   The Library
                     University College Dublin
                     Belfield
                     Dublin 4

Telephone   (01) 706 7686/ 706 7149

Enquiries to   The Special Collections Librarian

Opening hours   10.00–1.00, 2.00–5.00, Mon–Fri; by appointment;
and facilities   photocopying; photography; microfilming by arrange-
                     ment

Guides   Introductory leaflet

Major collections

Some papers relating to the movement for national independence, Irish language and local history, and early 20th century Anglo-Irish literature.
Includes letters and papers of and relating to Gerard Manley Hopkins
(1845–89), James Joyce (1882–1941), Patrick Kavanagh (1904–67),
Thomas Kettle (1880–1916), Henry Morris (Énrí Ó Muirgheasa)
(1874–1945), John O'Donovan (1809–61), Seán Ó Ríordáin (1916–77),
William Reeves (1815–92), Jack Butler Yeats (1871–1957); Mary Lavin
(1912–96); novels and plays of Maeve Binchy; plays, poems and short
stories of Frank McGuinness (1953–).
Minute books of the council of the Irish Academy of Letters, 1932–70.

University College Galway *see* National University of Ireland, Galway

235 University of Ulster Library at Coleraine

Address   Coleraine
                     County Londonderry BT52 1SA

Telephone   (01265) 44141

Fax   (01265) 324928

Enquiries to   The Librarian

Opening hours   9.00–10.00, Mon–Fri, 9.30–1.00 Sat during term;
and facilities   9.30–5.30 Mon–Fri during vacation;
                 photocopying; photography by arrangement

Major collections

Papers of George Shiels (1881–1949), playwright; Denis Johnston (1901–84), playwright and author; John Hewitt (1907–87) poet, Francis Stuart (1902–), novelist; George Stelfox (1884–1972), naturalist; E. Norman Carrothers (1898–1977), botanist and railway engineer.

Headlam-Morley collection of World War I material.

Paul Ricard collection of World War II material.

236   University of Ulster Library at Magee College

Address   Magee College
           Northland Road
           Londonderry BT48 7JL

Telephone   (01504) 371371

Enquiries to   Librarian

Opening hours   9.00–9.00, Mon–Fri, 10.00–1.00 Sat during term;
and facilities   9.00–5.00, Mon–Fri during vacation; photocopying

Major collections

A small collection of manuscripts, mainly 18th and 19th century in origin, with an emphasis on sermons and Presbyterian history but including some items of a more general historical interest.

237   Valuation Office

Address   Block 2
           Irish Life Centre
           Abbey Street Lower
           Dublin 1

| Telephone | (01) 817 1000 |
| Fax | (01) 817 1180 |

| Enquiries to | The Secretary |

| Opening hours and facilities | 9.30–12.30, 2.00–4.30, Mon–Fri; photocopying |

Major collections
Griffiths Primary Valuation, *c.*1852, for the Republic of Ireland with accompanying maps. Records of the Valuation List, 1852–, showing occupiers of properties.

238 Vincentian Fathers (Congregation of the Mission)Irish Province

| *Address* | St Peter's Phibsborough Dublin 7 |

| *Telephone* | (01) 838 9708 |

| *Fax* | (01) 838 9950 |

| *E-mail* | VINPHIBS@iol.ie |

| *Enquiries to* | The Archivist at (01) 283 6731 |

| *Opening hours and facilities* | By arrangement; photocopying |

| *Guides* | Thomas Davitt CM, 'The archives of the Irish Province of the Congregation of the Mission', *Catholic Archives* 5 (1985) |

Major collections
Material relating to the history of Vincentians in Ireland, Britain, China and Nigeria; to personnel; to St Vincent de Paul; to the general history of the Vincentians and to prominent individual non–Irish Vincentians, 1833–. Includes manuscript and typescript accounts of persons, events and ministries; as well as theses, notebooks, sermon books, account books, correspondence and a collection of published books and pamphlets of Vincentian interest.

239   Waterford City Archives

Address	City Hall The Mall Waterford
Telephone	(051) 843123
Fax	(051) 879124
E-mail	archives@waterfordcorp.ie
Website address	www.waterfordcorp.ie
Enquiries to	The City Archivist
Opening hours and facilities	By appointment; photocopying
Guides	*The Royal Charters of Waterford* (Waterford Corporation, 1992); Donal Moore 'Waterford City Archives. A New Service' in *Decies* 54

Major collections

The Liber Antiquissimus, 1365–1649; the Scroll of Richard II, *c.*1390; the Royal Charters (20 items), 1449–1815; records of the Council, 1655–1992.

Records of the Urban Sanitary Authority, 1874–1911; Waterford and New Ross Port Sanitary Authority, 1904–49; Committees of the Corporation, 1778–1945; Town Clerk, 1377–1992; Engineer's Office, 1834–1960; Estate Office, 1700–1970, including expired leases, 1663–1970s; Finance Office, 1796–1958; Motor Tax Office, 1903–70s; Planning files, 1948–79; Housing survey, 1939.

Small and private collections including Thomas Francis Meagher material, White's Chemist, Michael Walsh Asylum & Shea Institution, Waterford Music Club, Arts Advisory Committee, 1598–1980s.

Maps, plans and drawings, 1750s–1980s.

Photographs, 1870s–1990s.

Original data relating to archaelogical digs in the city, 1986–92.

240   Waterford County Archives Service

Address	Dungarvan Library Building, Davitt's Quay, Dungarvan Waterford

Telephone	(058) 41231
Enquiries to	County Librarian
Opening hours and facilities	By appointment; photocopying

Major collections

Archives of Waterford County Council, 1899–1960, and of predecessor bodies including the Grand Jury, 1829–99; Board of Guardians minute books for Waterford, 1848–1920, Lismore, 1843–1924, Dungarvan, 1849–1922, Kilmacthomas, 1851–1921. Archives of the Rural District Councils of Carrick-on-Suir, 1922–25, Lismore, 1899–1925, Waterford, 1899–1925, Dungarvan, 1899–1925, Kilmacthomas, 1899–1921, Clonmel, 1899–1925, and Youghal, 1889–1925.

Private paper collections including the Lismore Castle papers, 1625–1966; Chearnley papers, 1671–1911; papers relating to Mothel and Carrick-on-Suir; miscellaneous deeds relating to County Waterford.

241 Wesley Historical Society Irish Branch – Belfast

Address	Aldersgate House 13 University Road Belfast
Telephone	(01247) 815959
E-mail	WHS~@hotmail.com
Enquiries to	The Honorary Archivist
Opening hours and facilities	9.00–12.30, Thursdays and by appointment
Guides	*Bulletin* of the Wesley Historical Society (Irish Branch)

Major collections

Methodist Church in Ireland: Wesleyan Conference agenda and minutes as published, 1878–; Wesleyan Conference minutes, 1752–1878; Primitive Wesleyan Methodist Conference, 1818–78.

Methodist periodicals: *The Methodist Magazine* (Irish edition), 1801–22 (monthly with portraits of Irish preachers); *The Primitive Wesleyan Methodist Magazine,* 1823–78 (bi–monthly); *The Irish Evangelist,* 1859–83 (monthly); *Christian Advocate,* 1823–1923 (weekly); *Irish*

Christian Advocate, 1923–71 (weekly); *Methodist Newsletter*, 1973– (monthly).

Microfilms of Methodist registers of Northern Ireland circuits.

Miscellaneous: writings of Methodists (correspondence, diaries, scrapbooks), photographs and other illustrative material, late 18th–20th century.

242 Wesley Historical Society Ireland Branch – Dublin

Address	Wesley House
	Leeson Park
	Dublin 6
Enquiries to	The Archivist
Opening hours and facilities	By appointment only

Major collections

Records of some circuits and chapels (but not records of baptisms and marriages) in Dublin, 1820–.

243 Westmeath County Library

Address	County Library Headquarters
	Dublin Road
	Mullingar
	County Westmeath
Telephone	(044) 40781/2/3
Fax	(044) 41322
Enquiries to	The County Librarian
Opening hours and facilities	9.30–1.00; 2.00–5.00, Mon–Fri; photocopying
Guides	Marian Keaney, *Westmeath local studies: a guide to sources* (Mullingar, Longford/Westmeath Joint Library Committee, 1981); *Mullingar Branch Library Guide* (leaflet); *Athlone Branch Library Guide* (leaflet).

Major collections

Grand Jury: presentment books, 1842–99.

Board of Guardian material: Athlone Union, minute books, 1849–1920; abstract of guardians accounts, 1905–21; financial and statistical minute book, 1907–08. Mullingar Union, minute books, 1857–1921; daily diet book, 1857–58; cream account book, 1867–68; general ledgers, 1909–23.

Rural District Council minute books: Athlone No. 1 RDC minute books, 1899–1925; ledgers, 1915–25; rate books, 1923–45. Coole RDC minute books, 1899–1925; loans expenditure book, 1908–16; general ledgers, 1919–25; rate books, 1923–45. Mullingar RDC minute books, 1899–1925; waterworks committee minute book, 1905–22; rate books, 1905–45; personal ledger, 1907–25. Ballymore RDC minute books, 1900–25; register of separate charges, 1904–24; general ledgers, 1905–25; seed and manure supply scheme collection account books, 1918; rate books, 1922–45. Kilbeggan RDC minute books, 1914–17. Delvin RDC minute books, 1919–23; general ledger, 1923–25; rate books, 1923–45.

Board of Health records: county board of health and public assistance (County Home and Hospitals) minute books, 1921–42; contractor's ledger, 1934–43; medical assistance register, Athlone dispensary district, 1935–55; public assistance ledger, 1943–46.

County Council material: valuation lists, 1878–1972; registers of mortgages, 1880–1954; financial records, 1899–1967; minute books, 1899–1988; roads committee minute book, 1912–26; county surveyor's statement of expenditure on works, 1912–32; tuberculosis committee financial statement receipt book, 1918–20; housing maintenance ledger, 1922–28; labourers cottages rent collection books, 1923–71; register of motor cars, 1925–57; tuberculosis advisory committee minute book, 1926–34; attendance register, 1926–35; salary registers, 1927–40; storekeeper's stock book, 1928–43; sewerage, waterworks and burial board minute book, 1928–40; register of driving licences, 1932–75; manager's orders, 1942–77; registers of purchaser's cottages, 1944–56; manager's orders, joint library committee, 1945–88; engineering files, 1948–56; home assistance and expenditure books, 1949–68; grant reconstruction books, 1952–78; rent collection books, 1970–81;

Urban District Council minute books: Athlone UDC minute books, 1901–49; factories and workshops register, 1908–36; registers of cowkeepers and dairymen, 1908–70; rate books, 1911–76; artisans' dwellings rent collection books, 1913–66; poor rate book, 1914; waterworks and sanitary committee minute book, 1914–37; housing minute books, 1923–40; letter books, 1924–37; financial minute books, 1930–37; valuation lists, 1930–52; sanitary officer's report book,

1931–39; housing ledgers, 1933–59; financial statement books, 1933–78; postage book, 1939–48; manager's orders, 1942–60; ledgers of public slaughter houses, 1949–65; combined stock record books, 1949–72; water rent book, 1951–80; waterworks manager's log book, 1958–67.

Town Commissioners: Mullingar Town Commissioners minute books, 1923–57; financial statement records, 1930–73; artisan's dwellings general rentals, 1933–70; rate books, 1937–46; artisan's dwellings rent collection books, 1958–70; postage book, 1960–77.

Trustees of River Deel Drainage Board: minute book, 1869–1945; maintenance rate book, 1923–34.

Upper Inny Drainage Committee: minute book, 1932–40.

Small collection of private material including various rent books, 1816–1924; Athlone Loan Fund Society, 1865–1948.

Sources for local studies including material relating to Westmeath families and writers including Brinsley McNamara, Pakenham family, Fr Paul Walsh, Olive Sharkey, Padraic O'Farrell and Leo Daly. Howard-Bury and Belvedere House Collections, 1800–1940s, from Colonel C.K. Howard-Bury, leader of the first Everest Expedition, and Rex B. Beaumont, Belvedere House, Mullingar.

John Broderick Collection consisting of the novelist's library with inscribed copies of the works of leading Irish and French writers, together with a small collection of literary correspondence.

John Charles Lyons of Ledeston printing press and items of major Westmeath interest printed on it.

Estate papers and maps; Westmeath County Infirmary minute books; collections of photographs, newscuttings and newspapers on microfilm.

John B. Burgess Collection, 1885–1960, containing Athlone directories, wills and deeds, church registers, and other printed matter of Athlone interest.

244   Wexford Corporation

Address	Municipal Buildings Wexford
Telephone	(053) 42611
Fax	(053) 45947
E-mail	doncurt@wexcorp.iol.ie

Website address	www.wexford.ie/authorities/wc/index.htn
Enquiries to	The Staff Officer and Assistant Staff Officer
Opening hours and facilities	9.00–1.00, 2.00–5.00, Mon–Fri; photocopying

Major collections
Minutes of Wexford Corporation, 1776–.
Copies of title documents, 17th century–.
'Lacey Book' and map: record of Corporate Estate by Thomas Lacey, Borough Treasurer, 1854.
Charter, 1846.

245   Wexford County Library

Address	Abbey Street Wexford
Telephone	(053) 65052
Fax	(053) 21097
E-mail	library.wexford@tinet.ie
Enquiries to	The County Librarian
Opening hours and facilities	2.30–5.30, Tue; 10.00–5.30, Wed–Fri; 10.00–1.00, Sat; appointment necessary; photocopying

Major collections
Miscellaneous County Wexford estate papers: maps, rentals and sales of rentals, 1825–1908.
Wexford Harbour Board: minutes, accounts, cash books; transactions relating to registered ships, 1830–1907; ship arrivals and departures from Wexford Harbour 1831–9, 1904–22; log book for Pilot Boat, 1930–61; Light Ship records, 1919–29.
Specifications for St Ives Harbour, Cornwall, 1868.
Minute book of Primrose League Ardcandrisk Habitation No. 1084, 188696.
Wexford Tate School accounts, 1895 & 1897–1911.
Ferrycarrig Bridge: interest on Carrig Bridge debentures, 1823–72.
Photocopy of survey of the parishes of Clone, Kilbride, & Ferns, 16 May 1776.
Photocopy of miscellaneous letters of Colclough family, *c.*1800 and a copy of a transcript of the Declaration of Charles II in relation to the Colclough estate.
Typed copy of Samuel Barber's notes on Enniscorthy in 1798.

246   Wexford County Museum

Address	Castle Hill Enniscorthy Wexford
Telephone	(054) 35926
Fax	(054) 35926
E-mail	wexmus@iol.ie
Enquiries to	The Honorary Secretary
Opening hours and facilities	10.00–6.00, June–Oct; 2.00–5.30, Feb–May

Major collections

Letters, maps, deeds, miscellaneous papers referring mostly to the 1798 and 1916 rebellions in County Wexford.

247   Wicklow County Library

Address	UDC Offices Boghall Road Bray County Wicklow
Telephone	(0404) 61732
Enquiries to	The Archivist
Opening hours and facilities	By appointment only; photocopying

Major collections

Grand Jury presentments; Wicklow County Council minutes; Board of Guardians minutes, 19th century; Bray Urban District Council minutes; Rural District Council minutes of Shillelagh and Rathdrum; Wicklow Board of Health and Public Assistance minutes; Wicklow Urban District Council minutes; Poor Law Union minutes for Shillelagh and Rathdrum.

248   Wicklow Harbour Commissioners

Address	North Quay Wicklow
Telephone	(0404) 67455
Fax	(0404) 67455
Enquiries to	The Secretary
Opening hours and facilities	By appointment; photocopying

Major collections

Minute books, 1897–1954; damp press letter books, 1908–27; harbour dues and tolls, 1891–1965; account books, receipt books and pay orders, 1854–1970; correspondence, deeds, leases, maps and drawings.

249   Wilson's Hospital School

Address	Multyfarnham County Westmeath
Telephone	(044) 71115
Fax	(044) 71563
E-mail	WILSONSH@iol.ie
Website address	www.iol.ie/~wilsonsh
Enquiries to	The Bursar
Opening hours and facilities	By appointment; photocopying

Major collections

Registers of old men and boys, 1761–1923; registers of pupils, 1923–45, roll books, 1886–.

National School records: roll books, 1898–1946; daily report books, 1898–1938.

Weekly accounts, 1836–9, 1842–5, 1848–52, 1857–63, 1943–9, 1966–74; Wardens' accounts, 1895–1967.

Minutes of the Trustees and Guardians, 1913–6

Appendix 1

The following organisations have indicated that they hold archives but are unable at the present time to provide access of any sort to their holdings.

Augustinian House of Studies, Ballyboden, Dublin 16
Carmelite Order, Ballinteer, Dublin 16
Daughters of Charity of St Vincent de Paul, Blackrock, County Dublin
Ferns Diocesan Archives
National Women's Council of Ireland
St John of God Sisters, Wexford
Strokestown Park House, County Roscommon
University of Limerick

Appendix 2

The following organisations provided entries for one or both of the previous editions of this *Directory*. The custody of their archives has since been transferred to the institutions indicated.

Bantry House: National University of Ireland, Cork, Boole Library
Castletown House: in the temporary custody of the Irish Architectural Archive
Down & Dromore and Connor Diocesan Library: Public Record Office of Northern Ireland
Meath Diocesan Registry: Representative Church Body Library, Dublin
Office of Public Works: National Archives
Ordnance Survey: National Archives
Public Record Office of Ireland: National Archives
Royal Zoolological Society of Ireland: Trinity College Library Dublin, Manuscripts Department
St Canice's Cathedral Library, Kilkenny: Representative Church Body Library, Dublin
St Patrick's Cathedral, Dublin: Representative Church Body Library, Dublin
State Paper Office: National Archives

Appendix 3

Related organisations and institutions

Association of Church Archivists of Ireland

Honorary Secretary: Sr Marie Bernadette O'Leary
                         Religious Sisters of Charity
                         CARITAS
                         15 Guilford Road
                         Sandymount
                         Dublin 4

Telephone: (01) 269 7833
Fax: (01) 260 3085

Founded in 1980 as the Association of Religious Archivists of Ireland; present title adopted in 1992; holds regular meetings; organises occasional short training courses and workshops; membership open to anyone involved with religious archives of any denomination.

Association of Professional Genealogists in Ireland

                         c/o Genealogical Office
                         2 Kildare Street
                         Dublin 2

Fax: (01) 662 1062

Acts as a regulating body to maintain standards among its members and protect the interests of clients. Members bound by the APGI code of practice, undertake fee-paid genealogical research. Brochure and list of members available.

Irish Manuscripts Commission

                         73 Merrion Square
                         Dublin 2

Telephone: (01) 676 1610

Established in 1928 to report on and publish significant manuscript material; publishes the journal *Analecta Hibernica;* members appointed by the Minister for Arts, Heritage, Gaeltacht and the Islands.

Irish Society for Archives

Honorary Secretary: Mr Kieran Hoare
James Hardiman Library
National University of Ireland
Galway

Telephone: (091) 524411 ext 3636
Fax: (091) 522394
E-mail: kieran@sulacco.library.ucg.ie

General interest organisation founded in 1970 to promote awareness on all matters relating to archives in Ireland; organises a lecture series and publishes the journal *Irish Archives*; membership open to all.

National Archives Advisory Council

73 Merrion Square
Dublin 2.

Established under the provisions of the National Archives Act, 1986, to advise the Taoiseach in the exercise of his powers under the Act and on all matters affecting archives and their use by the public; Taoiseach's powers now devolved to the Minister for Arts, Heritage, Gaeltacht and the Islands to whom the Council submits an annual report which is laid before the Houses of the Oireachtas; twelve members appointed by the Minister.

Society of Archivists Irish Region

Honorary Secretary: Zoë Smyth
Acquisitions Section
Public Record Office of Northern Ireland
66 Balmoral Avenue
Belfast BT9 6NY

Telephone: (01232) 255836
E-mail: zoesmyth@hotmail.com

The professional body in the United Kingdom and Ireland for archivists, records managers and conservators; organised on a regional basis with special interest groups drawn from the total membership; represents the interests of the profession, sets professional standards, monitors and recognises training courses, and maintains a professional register; meetings held regularly at regional and national level; Irish Region has published *Standards for the development of archives services in Ireland* (1997); Society publishes the *Journal of the Society of Archivists* and a series of *Best Practice Guidelines*.

University College Dublin Archives Department
University College Dublin
Belfield
Dublin 4

Telephone: (01) 706 7545
Fax: (01) 706 1146
E-mail: ailsa.holland@ucd.ie

Provides a one-year, full-time postgraduate Higher Diploma in Archival Studies (HDipAS), a professional qualification recognised by the Society of Archivists; information available at www.ucd.ie/~archives; detailed prospectus available from the department.

Index

The numbers refer to the Directory number.